FIND THE WIND

by Jeanette Pickering

Vabella Publishing
P.O. Box 1052
Carrollton, Georgia 30112

Copyright © 2013 by Jeanette Pickering

All rights reserved. Except for brief quotes that may be used by a reviewer, no portion of any entry in this book may be duplicated or reproduced in any form, stored in any retrieval system or transmitted by any means in any format for any reason without written permission from this author.

13-digit ISBN 978-1-983230-51-6

Library of Congress Control Number 2013922073

10 9 8 7 6 5 4 3 2 1

DEDICATION

To title a book or a chapter in a book takes some thought and time. At least for me it does. But the title for this book came in an instant, long before the seed was ever planted.

One summer day when cousin Marillyn had come to visit, I was busy hanging a large, lovely, deep-toned wind chime that I had purchased while on a trip in Texas. First I hung it on the porch rafter. Then I moved it out to a tree limb by the shed. Nothing. No sound. No wind.

As I dragged the step ladder around to the corner of the house to fasten a screw to the roof overhang, Marillyn called out "What are you doing?"

"I'm trying to find the wind!"

Somehow I knew right then I would someday write a book and that its title would be "Find the Wind". But it took Marillyn's off-hand question to give it birth.

Thus to my beloved cousin who has always been my best friend, I dedicate this book to her.

TABLE OF CONTENTS

Preface
Introduction 1
Chapter 1 - Flight to St. Thomas P 4
Chapter 2 - Falling in Love 9
Chapter 3 - Preparing for a Hurricane 13
Chapter 4 - The Spanish Virgin Islands 17
Chapter 5 - White Sand Beaches 20
Chapter 6 - An Ending with thoughts of a New Beginning 24
Chapter 7 - Turkey Hollow Transpirings 28
Chapter 8 - Blue Cat Eye Earrings 32
Chapter 9 - The Captains Rules 36
Chapter 10 - A wedding Ring from a Gum Ball Machine 40
Chapter 11 - Ten Days in Culebra 44
Chapter 12 - Work and Play, All in One Day 48
Chapter 13 - An Eight Countdown 52
Chapter 14 - The Keeping of Written Thoughts 58
Chapter 15 - And We Pledged Ourselves P 62
Chapter 16 - Good Days, Bad Days, Swiftly Passing Days 66
Chapter 17 - October's End 71
Chapter 18 - A Face to Face Visit with GOD 75
Chapter 19 - A Tree in the Middle of the Road 79
Chapter 20 - Carib Indian Petroglyphs 83
Chapter 21 - Fin Fun on a Sunny Day 87
Chapter 22 - A Full Moon Sail 91
Chapter 23 - How to Be a Captain's Wife 96
Chapter 24 - A Garden of Botanical Beauty 101
Chapter 25 - Flamingos in a Harbor 105
Chapter 26 - Starfish Frisbees 109
Chapter 27 - Cemetery by the Sea 113
Chapter 28 - Clothing Optional 117
Chapter 29 - A Puerto Rican Parting 122

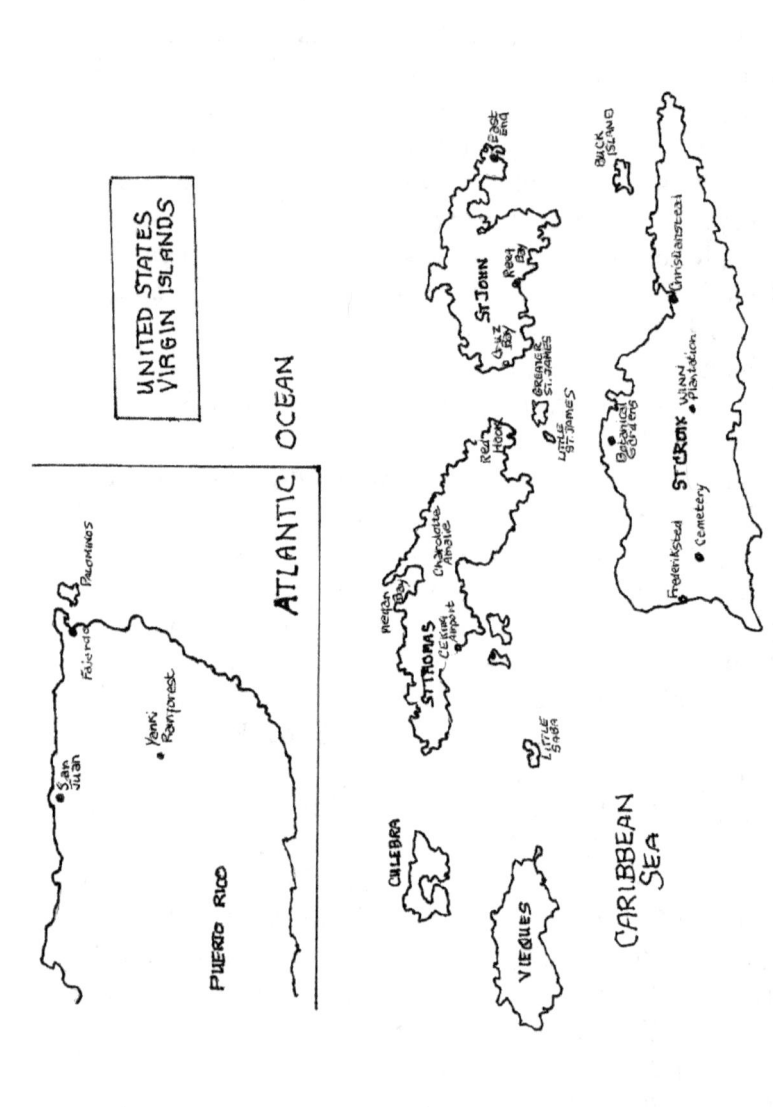

PREFACE

Every story must have a beginning, even if it's only a simple "once upon a time". But before I start at the beginning of this story I should tell you, there are clues hidden in among the words of this travelogue fairy tale that hint of its ending. As you follow along with me while I search to find and then follow the wind, you will be the one who determines if this is a mythical golden love story or a cautionary, sometimes bitter-tinted tale. It could even be both. You will have to judge for yourself.

In any case, this story developed and grew as most of our lives often do; with ups and downs, twists and turns, joys and sorrows and then more joy. Yet the roller-coaster ride I experienced was mine. And I enjoyed it beyond measure.

And now to begin.

INTRODUCTION

HOW IT ALL BEGAN

The Princess Cruise Liner that was to take me to see a new world, extended out to include all and more than I could have expected. The group that I was traveling with had boarded her in Acapulco, Mexico after having flown across parts of two continents to reach her. The local bus ride from the airport gave me a foretaste of similar adventures of travel that I would experience in the next few years. A dirty-windowed small bus plowed through the crowded traffic of narrow streets on a Sunday afternoon in October 1998 as it circled around the bay to the wharf where the Liner was docked.

I had experienced the checking in and out of customs and immigration offices earlier this spring while traveling to Australia and New Zealand, so I partially knew what to expect in processing the papers needed. But it was the immensity of the boat, practically a city in itself, and the exhilaration of knowing I would be sailing to places I had only dreamed I would ever see, that kept me awake on that humid evening that reeked with the smell of salty sea air.

At midnight the Liner's huge air horns signaled with their regulated five blasts, letting all who could hear know that we were leaving the harbor and that the adventures had begun. As the city lights and sounds trailed off behind us I stood at the railing on the deck and let my thoughts drift into the darkness above the inky sea.

"You've come a long way, Jeanette. Years spent raising your family, working in a profession of caring for the dead and their grieving families, facing grief yourself first hand in caring for your dying husband of forty-seven years and eventually burying him. Can you now finally let go of the struggling sorrow and find a joy that will fill you with a future of simple happiness? Relax. Enjoy what you can, while you can."

It was on the second day out before I could really begin to relax. We had arrived on the Pacific side of Costa Rica where we boarded a big bus that took us on a wild ride up a narrow two-lane mountainous road through the heart of Costa Rica, finishing out the trip with a tour of the no-street-signs city of San Jose. A few days later, we crossed the American continent through the Panama Canal and visited Cartagena, Columbia, to celebrate the 506th anniversary date of Columbus's discovery of the new world. The Cruise Liner stopped on the island of Aruba where we hurried through an interesting but very small island inhabited by Dutch, German, French, Portuguese and native Indians. A day later we made a trip through the island of St. Martins which led us through two different countries. We traveled the Dutch side first and then on to the French side where we stopped for a small boat snorkel sail. It was here I encountered my first eye-popping nude beach, chatting while clothed in my bathing suit with a large gentleman enjoying the sun in his birthday suit.

But it was the next day that my world as I had known it, became up-ended. Let me share with you a small excerpt from my Daily Journal:

"FRIDAY, October 16, 1998

I had to get up early today. We are to have our passports stamped and pick up our airline tickets for tomorrow's departure. After getting a bite to eat I got in line for the side trip tour of St. Thomas and a sail boat/snorkel excursion. It was a beautiful day as we sailed out to Buck Island. The time passed swiftly as I enjoyed the snorkel adventure. I found a sand dollar and handed it up to the Captain to keep for me until we were ready to go. (Then I forgot and left it on the boat.) On our way back to the Cruise Liner I visited with the crew: Jeff, the mate who had tattoos on his arms and Captain Dennis who wore his on his legs. Ah, what can I say about Dennis…he asked me to come and live with him. And he changed my life."

Little did I know on that day when I exchanged addresses with this charming and extraordinary Captain that two years later I would also exchange wedding vows with him. For it took that long for us to share our thoughts and dreams through our letters to finally arrive at a place where we both knew we wanted to spend the rest of our lives together.

CHAPTER ONE

FLIGHT TO ST. THOMAS, U S V I

During the next two years the silver fountain pen I had purchased on one of my previous travels got a good workout. Letters scratched out in a notebook and then transferred in my finest penmanship on proper stationary were mailed out weekly. And as time passed Dennis' and my casual and interesting friendship slowly and cautiously made its way into a romantic one.

So it really wasn't a big surprise to me when on the first day of August 2000, the call came from St. Thomas. This was a bold new Dennis asking me to come and spend a couple of weeks with him on his boat. In all the time we had exchanged letters, I had received only two photos of him. None of his boat. Yes, I am a curious person, so I am surprised that I had never asked to see a picture of the boat he had described in his letters. I had no idea what it looked like. Most of what we wrote about was ourselves, our families, his work and his summer trips to Alaska. So staying on a boat that I knew nothing about, I felt might be a bit of a challenge. Why I didn't ask more pertinent, personal questions when his call came, I don't know. All I knew was that something good was happening here. I had no doubts. I was not afraid. And I wanted to go.

The next day I bought a round-trip ticket to St. Thomas to arrive on August 15th. The letter writing was now a daily delight. A day later he called again. After I had hung up I scolded myself for acting like such a silly school girl, bewitched by her first love. When I told my children what I was going to do, eyebrows went up. But delight and envy filled the grandchildren.

I knew they all were discussing this latest escapade of mine as a bit 'off-base'. "She's an old woman for goodness sake. She'll be seventy years old next month. Taking off to go sailing with a, 'how old did she say he was? Forty-eight?' year old man on a boat two thousand miles away?"

But there was nothing to suggest that I would be murdered or sold off as a foreign slave, so with a shrug of their shoulders and a "Whatever makes you happy", they wished me well. The granddaughters helped me go shopping for new clothes.

I had chosen a purple dress as the one in which to meet Dennis for the second time. The romantic woman in me chose it for the way I felt whenever I wore purple. A bit royal, a smidgeon guarded, a tad shy and with a drop or two of serenity and maturity.

The practical woman that also lived in me chose it because it was comfortable and needed very little grooming attention. The car trip to the airport and the long plane ride would take its toll on any garment that I might choose, not even considering that there would be a problem of how to fold and store it when I did arrive. The dress had been purchased shortly after my widowhood began and on this day hung quite fetchingly over my hundred-twenty pound, seventy year old frame.

The days flew by fast. On the Tuesday morning of August 15th, I woke at 4:00 a.m. One of my sons was to drive me to the airport. He never came. He had forgotten he was to take me. So I drove myself and left my car in the long term parking. The excitement of it all had made my legs wobbly. Yet I finally got seated in the plane for the 8:15 departure and immediately fell limp with relief. I had made it this far at least. Now that I could not back out, the doubts that I had not allowed to creep in, crept in. And for a spell they niggled at me as the plane droned over the southern states.

When the plane left the U.S. mainland and began its afternoon flight over the intense blue waters of the Atlantic Ocean, I watched as the water changed its color from blue to green. In Puerto Rico I was transferred to a smaller plane which flew at a lower altitude, allowing me to view the dots of larger islands that were surrounded by specks of smaller islands. Though by now, the earlier doubts had dissolved.

At 4:50 p.m. the plane taxied across the small St. Thomas runway. Climbing out of the cool air conditioned cabin, the strength of the hot humid tropic air caught my breath. I maintained a sensation of gliding as I walked alongside the glass wall of the St. Thomas terminal. I could not see in for the brightness of the Caribbean sun had almost blinded me. Could he see me? What would he be thinking? Would I please him? I felt confident that I would or he would never have called to invite me. It had taken him two years. That's a long time for someone to mull things over and make up one's mind. It was for me.

The perpetually open entrance, wide to accommodate all the many travelers that arrive at this airport, reverberated with the sounds of the tropics. Calypso music was playing over the loud speakers. The voices of the native cab drivers were loud as they tried to divert new customers to their vans. The antiquated luggage rack rumbled as it rotated on its orbit from the outside to inside and then back outside.

The air was heated with a strange, continuous soft pressure. It could almost talk, saying "I am here for the duration of your trip. Get used to me for I don't go away". But I liked the feel of it. No, I loved the feel of it. It was exciting to be caressed with this sweet warm breeze even when inside this open-air building. There were no coverings for the doors and windows to impede the gentle warm flow of that sweet sea born air. I was in a new world.

Would I know him? I had only two small photographs and a faint memory of what he looked like. The photographs had been viewed and perused and searched a thousand times for a hint of knowledge of who this man might really be. His letters could give me clues but still could not disclose even a fraction of the real character of this man that was waiting for me somewhere in the crowd.

And then I saw him. He stood there with a twinkle in his blue eyes and a welcoming grin on his tanned face, holding up a sign reading "JEANETTE FOR S/V ROSA SALVAJE WITH CAPT. DENNIS". (I still have the sign.) He was so handsome. I walked straight to him as if I had known him forever and placed my arms around his neck, kissing him on his lips as if I had done so a thousand times before. All doubts were gone. I knew I had done the right thing to come here.

ROSA was anchored in the Bay beside the airport. It took two dinghy trips to get my luggage to the boat. Years later he recalled those moments. "Did you ever realize how very vulnerable you were right then? I had left you standing there on that beach, barefoot and alone, with everything you had brought with you now on my boat. I thought you to be the bravest woman I had ever met. I knew then that we belonged together."

I could see that I had brought way too much luggage. I changed out of my purple dress into shorts and a tank top. We motored to Honeymoon Bay where we ate a supper of ham, pineapple, corn and salad, cooked by Dennis. It would be the last meal he would prepare for us

FIND THE WIND

for a long time. After our meal he motored over to land to make a phone call to his employer. They had a charter sail scheduled to go out tomorrow so we left the Bay and motored back to his regular mooring spot near the Cruise Ships where we spent a beautiful evening together."

I had made my peace with what was to follow. The knowledge that others might never be able to understand the choices I had just made for my future, would always rest within me. But I had come from the back of the wind to find the reason for my living. And I had found him.

August 15, 2000

Jeanette by the sign 'Welcome to St. Thomas'

CHAPTER TWO

FALLING IN LOVE

For the next week Dennis went to work each day taking a new group of Cruise Ship passengers out to Buck Island, just as he had taken me and other passengers of our group almost two years before. I stayed on *ROSA* trying to get acclimated to her tiny living quarters. I had not expected such a small cramped boat, but I had no problem in adjusting. I was enjoying Dennis and being in his company allowed me to overlook a lot of things. I found that the motion of the boat didn't adversely affect me as it does some people, including Dennis. For a sailor he experienced sea-sickness quite often in our sailing travels. The fact was I felt the motion to be quite soothing.

I always had supper ready when he got home for he usually didn't have time to eat lunch. He was scheduled for two trips a day; out and back, morning and afternoon. Of course all his friends dropped by to meet me. Boat neighbors are a lot like land neighbors; wondering just what kind of a person would come stay with Dennis for two weeks.

Dennis had asked for Thursday off to show me places of interest on the island. But before we left the boat, we spent the morning going over some of the things that are imperative in making *ROSA* safe and workable. A floating house is quite different than a stable, unmoving land home. Learning the ins and outs of toilet stool flushing required me to make notes until I could remember for sure which valve to open while the other was closed. If both were opened at the same time you had better pump the handle fast or you quickly had an overflow problem. My thoughts that day were "I'm not sure I could handle this for a long period of time." Yet there were lots of folks in this harbor that were doing just that.

I was flattered by all his attention as we took a Maxi Taxi down into the tourist shopping district. We went to the old Fort that was built along the bay and poked around through the museum. I felt myself becoming more infatuated with this man and I truly seemed to forget there was even an age difference between us. As we walked through the garden passageways between the buildings we laughed and teased. Dennis bought me a wrap-around Caribbean skirt which I put on when we got back to the boat. We talked about our families, our lives. Way up into the night we talked. We couldn't seem to get enough of sharing our stories face to face. Always before it was limited to letter conversations.

On Saturday Dennis stopped by the boat at lunch time for a quick sandwich, and to tell me he had an evening tour. "Would you like to go with me?" "Sure!" So I cleaned up, put on a black outfit with a belt made from a piece of material Dennis had sent me a long time ago. He is amazed at my talents and is so proud of me. The evening sail didn't go out to Buck Island. This was only a motor trip around the Charlotte Amalie Harbor and Water Island. Tonight he had a mate named Scotty, a neat young boy who is a bit lost I think. Sailing, swimming and girls are about all he has on his mind. He is thinking about buying a boat and had asked Dennis's advice about what to get. I really enjoyed the evening, the sounds and smells of the tourist section of the harbor. Later we walked around the hotel where the office of the Tour Company that Dennis works out of is located.

Jeanette Pickering

Five days have already passed. It's all spinning by too fast. We have already become closely attached in our emotions. A strong feeling of not wanting it all to end has begun to creep in. What will the next week bring? Can we keep our feelings in tow or have they been bound together with a strength that we will not be able to break? I think I already know the answer...

August 19, 2000   Charlotte Amalie, St. Thomas

Jeanette in front of the St. Thomas Fort clock

CHAPTER THREE

PREPARING FOR A HURRICANE

On our first Sunday together we had made plans to attend worship services with a couple of Dennis's friends, Eadie and Denny. For the most part, the people I was now meeting were known only by their first names. Later on in our travels this tradition would prove to be confusing and would often require an additional qualifying name or initial.

We had clothed ourselves in our Sunday best and dinghied in to the dock where they were to pick us up. They had a car. Only it was Jimmy, Dennis's boss, who met us there with the news that a hurricane was on its way and Dennis was needed to help get all the charter boats taken to the boatyard, to be pulled from the water for protection. Dennis returned to *ROSA* to change his clothes. I went on to church with Eadie and Denny. It was a Pentecostal Church with most of the congregation being West Indians. Because everyone was so congenial and friendly, I had no problem feeling welcome. But the mannerisms of the Islanders took some getting use to. There was no haphazard dress code—everyone put on their finest. They dressed up to meet the Lord. Also I was to find that Island women wear hats to church, not hankies on the head but big, beautiful Hats.

After the services a friend motored me back out to the boat where I waited for Dennis. He was finished at 4:00 p.m. He had been discussing the hurricane with his friends. They advised me to leave the island, to catch a plane back home. But having never been in a hurricane before, I was curious, along with being fearful. Not being sure I should stay but also not wanting to go, I wore a false bravado and opted to stay. Some of his friends who used their own personal sailing vessels for what are called 'six-pack sails' (total capacity of six passengers to a trip) were going to sail their crafts west to the protected mangrove swamps on the island of Vieques. Dennis chose to do the same. So we took on fuel and water, filled the cooler with ice and sailed out at dusk.

    This was to be my first long sail on *ROSA*. It was a beautiful night, the calm before the storm so to speak. I stayed up all night with Dennis, fascinated with the hundreds of procedures required just to maneuver the sailing sloop across the dark blue waters. I was to receive my first of a thousand sailing lessons. For every day there was a new rule, a new tack to the wind. And even if I used a five hundred page sailing book, there would still be something new to learn.

    It was daybreak before we entered into the various canals leading back to the safest area. We were the first ones in. The others had larger and faster boats so they could wait to make their passage during the next day. The U. S. has a Navy Base here on the eastern side of the island where the mangroves are. It has been used for years as a practice bombing range but because of a local protest, the base had stopped its operations. That was why we were allowed to come in.

    After a morning nap, we tied *ROSA* down in a small side pocket off the main artery. The water was cloudy and tannin colored so we did no swimming. When the others came in later during the day, Dennis went to help them tie their lines from their boat-cleats to the heaviest trunks of the mangrove trees. Since we would remain there for the next few days, I had a chance to become acquainted with a group of people who became almost like family to me. A few of them have remained in contact with me all through the years.

I have found that sailing people have to depend upon one another for their basic safety. Information of all sorts is shared in a multitude of ways. But the V H F radio is the most popular form of communication. And the most important lesson for me during that week we spent in the waters around Vieques Island was learning how to use our "Telephone."

August 21, 2000   Vieques Island

FIND THE WIND

Dennis in the dinghy tying up boat in Vieques Mangroves

CHAPTER FOUR

THE SPANISH VIRGIN ISLANDS

Hurricane Debbie chose only to be a teaser. A few high winds that howled as they swooshed through the mangroves. A steady downpour of rain. And a great reason to tuck into the shelter of *ROSA's* tiny cabin to enjoy each other's company.

By the next morning it had all passed, leaving a dinghy full of marvelously clean, unsalted water. Some of it was bailed out to be strained and added to the water tank. The rest was used for bathing. I wasn't quite ready to take a bath in a small, open boat but I could take a shower on the bigger one. I sat on the rounded closed hatch and with a drinking cup, dipped from a red three-gallon bucket to pour the soft rain water over me. Dennis sat and splashed away in the tiny boat like a two year old. All he lacked was a rubber ducky.

The fear that hurricanes can induce in people who live on the water kept everyone from untying just yet. An evening party was planned on the boat named *BEAR*. I found out that the owner, Chuck, had also lived in St.Joe, MO where we were both raised. We attended different schools but enjoyed the reminiscing of old times.

The following day the six-pack boats began to inch their way out of the mangroves and into the larger harbor basin. They needed to get back to work. It was low tide and some needed assistance as they had become stuck in the rich mud of the shallow water. It was on that day we met Terrie and Paul, a couple we would run into time and again on our travels south to Trinidad. After we had helped those who required a tug, the four of us explored the outer beaches of the island. It was a beautiful day, not even a hint of the hurricane that had slipped beyond and to the north of the Spanish Virgin Islands. We gathered shells and played in the ocean surf. It was a good day for photographs and I took quite a few. That evening when most had gathered in the outer harbor, planning for an early morning return, we visited on a different boat. I was quickly adapting to the ways of boat living, yet at the same time was making no permanent plans of making it a way of life. I was enjoying each day as it came; fellowshipping with people I found to be hard working, companionable and close knit in their boating relationships.

Only five more days of my vacation remained. Because *"SHADOW"*, the charter boat that Dennis worked on, was now in the boatyard, Dennis would not need to rush back to St. Thomas. We could use the next few days exploring a couple more of the islands in the vicinity. Culebra was the first on the way back. We anchored in the Dewey Harbor near the boat of Dennis's friend, Richard. He is building a box for Dennis that will be fastened to the stern railing and hold extra diesel fuel. The three of us shared a Pizza in a quaint Spanish speaking bar. The language spoken in all the Spanish Virgin Islands is of course, Spanish. And even though I had studied the language for two years while I was in High School, that was over fifty-two years ago. I had forgotten most of what I had learned and found I could barely converse with the locals. Dennis did much better. That evening he ordered ice cream cones which we took with us to the town plaza where we watched the island children as they roller bladed in and out of the streets.

How many times during the past few days have I had to stop and catch my breath. This couldn't be anything but a dream. Yet it was real. And something was happening inside of me. Something wonderful, yet a bit scary too. But as I let my breath out in a sweet sigh and reached for the hand of the second man in my life that could make me feel this way, I knew I was embarking on a sail into a wild, new, magical world of fresh adventure from which I might never return.

August 24, 2000   Culebra, SVI

Jeanette and Dennis on a beach in Vieques

CHAPTER FIVE

WHITE SAND BEACHES

Today I must call my family. I know they are concerned. And I do feel a little ashamed that the only word they have had from me was a call from the airport on the afternoon I arrived. Yet there is not one guilty pang in my heart. It is way too full of an awakened delight in being alive again.

There was a pay phone near the car rental place. Both Dennis and I made a call to our families. Later we picked up Richard in the rental car and made an exciting tour of this small Culebra Island. Richard has lived here for a number of years so he knew the interesting spots.

Whenever I've traveled in the past, I have always been curious to know about that country's traditions of burying their dead and visiting their cemeteries. I guess it's a throwback to my forty years of working in funeral service. So naturally I asked to see the ones on this island. There was only one, started many years ago on a steep hillside overlooking the bay rather than the sea. And instead of ground burials they use ornately decorated crypts.

We enjoyed the beautiful, fine white sand beach on the northern side where two old army tanks had been abandoned during WWII and left to rust. Some enterprising artist had painted one of them with extraordinary designs. After a fantastic lunch of greasy cheeseburgers and fries, we turned the rental car back into the place where we had picked it up. Close by was a Laundromat where we did some laundry. Just before we left to return to the boat, we purchased ice for tomorrows sail.

Even though we had arrived early the next morning on the small island of Culebrita, it was already crowded with boats from San Juan, Puerto Rico; people who had come over for a weekend excursion. We swam in the crystal clear water, giving me a chance to enjoy using an old snorkel mask Dennis had found somewhere. He used fins which added power to his swimming and we held hands as he pulled me with ease through the pale green water.

We used our oars rather than taking the time to attach the small out-board motor to the dinghy, to take us to shore where we hiked two miles up to an old lighthouse to view the sea. On the way up I found an irregularly shaped coconut. I brought it back to hang from *ROSA's* back stay where it rode out many windy storms. Many years later I hung it in the back bedroom of my home in Turkey Hollow as a reminder of a beautiful day when time stood still.

Spending a few moments at the top of the hill where the light house stands guard, I allowed myself a time to search my soul to try to understand what was happening to me. As I looked out over this vast Caribbean Sea, I saw that my newly acquired love for it was clashing with the knowledge that I would have to return to my land locked home on Tuesday. The anchorage on Culebrita only allowed day anchoring so we all had to return back to Culebra before sundown.

When I awoke the next morning, a beautiful sunrise greeted me. I spent some quiet time sitting on *ROSA's* round bow hatch cover. I wrote letters to my family and friends of the tremendous experiences I was enjoying. I was later joined on deck by Dennis. We spoke to one another of the thoughts that surrounded our unique and special relationship. No great plans were made but many personal and private words were shared, and vows were made including one which committed my eventual return to *ROSA* and her Captain. Once I returned to the states, there would be lots of preparation required before I could return to the sea.

    The return to St. Thomas was an unpleasant voyage because of the wild seas left in hurricane Debbie's wake. Dennis, even after all his long years of sailing, has the affliction of sea-sickness. He was required to run to the side of the boat a number of times during the trip to empty his stomach. He could not lie down but was forced to stay on his feet and on deck in order to get us back. I wasn't bothered with sea-sickness but I hadn't the faintest clue as to how to sail the boat either. It was very late when we finally moored *ROSA* in Long Bay. It had been a hard sail for Dennis, trimming the sails and keeping the ship on course without assistance from me. Oh my, I have so much to learn!

    August 27, 2000   St. Thomas, USVI

Jeanette Pickering

Jeanette and Dennis by the Army Tank in Culebra

CHAPTER SIX

AN ENDING WITH THOUGHTS OF A NEW BEGINNING

 Today would be our last full day to be together. Dennis was not ready to check back in at work yet, so we used our hours together getting away from the hub-bub and noise of the touristy Long Bay Harbor. We unfastened *ROSA* from her mooring and sailed out to a small island called Little Saba. It was a quiet, uninhabited island. On its western beach lay a lovely sailing vessel which had been washed up in a past hurricane. She was lying on her side, abandoned, with free salvaging for anyone who wanted anything. She had pretty well been scrapped out but still contained lots of lovely interior teak wood. Dennis chose to climb up the slanted mast to retrieve a part off of the radar unit.
 I walked the pea-sized-pebbled beach scavenging treasures. I found a nice black fender for Dennis to hang over the side of our boat to protect her from other boats banging against the hull. I had developed diarrhea during the night and since we had rowed in some distance from *ROSA* in the dinghy, I had no quick access to a private spot to relieve myself. Realizing my precarious situation, Dennis found some salvage material and quickly fashioned me a sided shelter for privacy. I was touched by his thoughtfulness, which endeared him to me all the more.
 Later in the warm, mellow afternoon we sailed back to the mooring with plans to spend our last evening on a 'date'. Dennis had chosen a fancy restaurant, high up on the hillside that overlooks Charlotte Amalie Harbor. I wore my black sun dress and pearls and felt elegantly

lady-like. The place was crowded so we had to wait a spell to get a table. The one where we were finally seated was in the center of the room. We were unable to see the bay or *ROSA*. We ordered and relished a great seafood meal, asking for a take home bag for the ample leftovers.

We poked along with our alloted time, not having any worries that would hurry us. When a table near the windows opened up, I saw Dennis go to a waitress, and slip her a bill. Within minutes we found our table service moved to the better location. This man knows how to wine and dine a woman, I'm thinking.

It was late when we took a taxi back to the dock and in our dreamy frame of minds, left those delicious leftovers in the taxi. Bummer!

We knew this would be our last night together, but I also knew I WOULD BE COMING BACK! As we quietly contemplated the up-coming separation, the excitement of the evening slowly softened down. We listened to a tape of soft Celtic music called 'Secret Gardens', and cried together.

My plane home was to leave at mid-morning. We had chosen not to sail to the bay by the airport and ferry the luggage back to the beach in the dinghy, for we would still have had to carry it quite a distance back to the terminal. Instead we took a taxi from the dock near our mooring and easily checked the luggage in. We found a bench outside where we could sit quietly to say our goodbyes. We have fallen in love. How long will it last? Who knows? But we both desperately want it to work. I now have a new reason for living, one worth the facing of my family with the news I will be moving back to St. Thomas.

The flight home was a meditative one. I napped a lot. The plane stopped in San Juan where I would have

FIND THE WIND

two more transfers, the final one landing in Springfield after dark. I retrieved my car from the lot and drove back to Turkey Hollow. The next day I called my cousin to tell her that she would not be able to come to Turkey Hollow for a visit in September as we had planned. And then I told her why. She was disappointed on both counts. Now, to inform my children...

      August 29, 2000   Turkey Hollow

Dennis climbing the mast on a boat on Little Saba

CHAPTER SEVEN

TURKEY HOLLOW TRANSPIRINGS

The two weeks I spent with Dennis had gone by so fast. Now, the next two waiting for the date of my departure back to the land of paradise, seemed to take forever to pass. There were moments when I felt as a teenager would and then in a few minutes I would turn to see myself as a crazy old fool.

I purchased the airline tickets. I did some banking. And I was able to skillfully talk to my children about Dennis and what I was doing. They mostly listened, offering very little advice but pointing out a few pertinent facts. Then they calmed what trepidation I may have felt, with a "Whatever you want to do will be O.K."

Wednesday was the third anniversary of Max's death. I purchased two red roses to take out to the Country Club where I placed them on the memorial bench that my family had erected there in Max's memory. It would be difficult for me to explain to them why two roses. I was struggling with it myself. But one rose was from me and the other from Dennis. As I spoke often about my deceased husband, he quickly adopted a deep respect for the gentle man I lived with for forty-seven years and asked if I would put one there for him also.

I took the many rolls of film I had taken to be printed. As I unpacked my suitcase, I laid out things I would be taking back. Only this time they would be packed in disposable cardboard boxes. My house was now a scrambled mess. All my house plants had wilted. But so what. I will soon be leaving them anyway to escape for the winter to sail with my lover.

The days moved along alternating good ones with bad ones. And easy ones. I called the R E A to change the payment method on my electric bill. I made arrangements with Missy to give me a permanent. I asked her if she would let me have my mail transferred to her so that she could pay my other bills and to once a month forward my letters by general delivery to whatever island I might be on. I made copies of my credit cards but planned to take only one with me.

I stopped delivery on my newspapers, resigned my office in the Garden Club, shopped for a portable iron that could be heated on *ROSA*'s gas stove burners and passed along the word to the many friends I ran into about what I was doing. Most were excited for me; some were leery. And rightly so. Everything had been all right with my children. Or so I thought. Yet a problem I should have expected arose to be discussed in depth. That of money. The incoming and outgoing of my finances. We worked it out wisely and amicably. I have never been more proud of my children than right then. I realized that they truly have a sound grip on the reality of life.

My biggest problem, which would not be a problem at all for many of this generation, developed within myself. Come Sunday morning, I was unable to face all those I would be worshiping with, knowing what I was now doing and what I planned to continue to do. So I stayed at home to share these final days before my departure with the grandchildren who had come to see me for a few days.

During the second week I went to Lebanon to take some basic computer lessons. I got my first e-mail address. The cost of phone calls home would prove to be very expensive from foreign islands. Dennis had explained that there are cyber-cafes on nearly every island that I could use. I also made arrangements with the bank to handle my business with them by computer.

Each day I either spoke to Dennis or wrote him a letter. He had found out he no longer had a tour guide job when he called in the day I left. They had expected him to return to the boat yard when the hurricane did not materialize, to scrape and paint their fleet of tour boats. Thus when he stayed that last week with me, they were plum peeved. He wasn't worried though. He knew we would be heading south to Trinidad just as soon as I returned.

He had spent the past two weeks on the island of St. Johns, putting up new lines and new sails he had ordered earlier this summer. He was so anxious for me to finally get back. The nagging fear that something unforeseen would come up was always there, waiting to trip us up. But we had decided that we would not be intimidated by doubts and think only positive thoughts. And so the days passed as I impatiently counted them off one by one.

September 15, 2009   Turkey Hollow

Jeanette Pickering

House in Turkey Hollow

CHAPTER EIGHT

BLUE CAT-EYE EARRINGS

I awoke at 3:30 to be ready for the 7:35 flight back to St. Thomas. It was extremely hard for me to leave my home knowing I wouldn't return until Christmas. I pushed hard to finish all the things that still needed to be done.

I talked to God a long time about what I was planning to do. I really opened up to Him for I didn't believe I could manage all this on my own. As usual He remained silent, dumping it all back in my lap. But I felt He was in this with me. I had found someone that loved me and everything would be O.K.

The flight was uneventful, arriving well after dark because of layovers. Dennis had moved *ROSA* to the east end so in his last phone call he had asked me to catch a taxi over to the Red Hook Ferry landing where he would meet me. I got the directions wrong and went to the Red Hook dock. I searched everywhere but was unable to find him. I became very frightened when a man with a push cart wanted to take my boxes from the taxi and go to the dock to hunt for the boat. I wouldn't let the Taxi driver leave until I could find Dennis. An older woman who seemed to be trustworthy said she would help me find him. And she did. He was waiting for me in front of the Yahoo Restaurant on the landing. I was relieved. Dennis thought it was humorous. I wasn't so sure. But I was way too tired to complain.

The boat had not been docked but anchored out. Even though the area was still noisy and the water rocky, we stayed. A storm had been forecast for the next few days so the following morning we went in to get groceries and ice. I also needed a pair of fins and a snorkel mask of my own. The ones I had previously used had been rented from the Havensite Dive Shop. At the Red Hook Dive shop a sweet young girl helped me pick out a pair of fins that would fit nicely over a pair of booties (to keep me from rubbing blisters on my tenderfoot feet. Just as we finished with our shopping a heavy rain began. We ducked into a bar where we ran into Dennis's friend Jeff, who often mated for him on his snorkel tours. Jeff had only one leg but was an excellent mate. He listened to Dennis as he blew out the story of how he had taught me to scuba dive by putting his gear on me, making me stand on the anchor and dropping it into the deep water. Jeff was aghast. He was so peeved at Dennis and took such compassion on me that he gave me the nice yellow tuna that he had caught that morning. I invited him to come eat it with us but he had other plans. I took compassion on Dennis and agreed to share it with him IF he would fillet it out for me. It turned out to be a nice sized slab of white meat.

    That evening the weather surprised us and cleared off so we motored out of Red Hook Bay, heading for an anchorage that Dennis felt was a safe place to ride out a storm. We had gotten a few miles out when the motor quit. He put up the sails and tried to sail the boat to Independent Boat Yard but had to go through a narrow pass that had a strong current heading out against us. He got the engine started again and we were to motor through the pass. It wasn't until we had gotten out of the strong current that we noticed a burning smell. Dennis quickly shut down the engine. Because the breeze was strong we were able to use the sail to get around to Christmas Cove on Little Saint James Island. We anchored with plans to spend some time there, maybe even a few days.

    To make sure the two anchors we had dropped would hold, Dennis dove down to secure them. I would later learn that this is a regular function that he performs each time we find an anchorage for *ROSA*.

Monday morning broke with a beautiful clear sky. The storm had dissipated during the night. Today I would celebrate my seventieth birthday. I fried ham and baked biscuits for Dennis in the tiny oven. He loved it. He also had two birthday presents for me. He gave me the first one after seeing me use the dish towel to take the biscuits from oven. It was an oven mitt made to look like some undescript animal that reminded me of an aardvark. I name him "Ardie" and pronounced him as my pet. He was never used as an oven mitt but poked his head from over the top of the radio speaker where he chased off any demons or dragons that might be lurking about the cabin.

Dennis had rowed to the beach that morning and had created a work of art with which to surprise me. He had placed various mid-sized stones and shells in the shape of a heart and constructed our two initials inside it. During the afternoon we swam over to the beach where he gave me the second gift. It was a pair of blue cat-eye earrings, bound in silver. I loved them and wore them for days.

It was a joyful day. Only one other boat came by. The sunset was fabulous. That evening I knew for sure I had done the right thing in coming back to this man and the new life that was about to open up for me.

September 18, 2000   St. Thomas USVI

Jeanette's birthday, with a shell heart on the beach

CHAPTER NINE

THE CAPTAIN'S RULES

The idyllic unfettered life could not continue forever. I had brought with me enough of my savings to go sailing for a spell and to see other Caribbean Islands. But even though we talked about what voyages we would make and what we would do, we were moving too slow for me. Dennis seemed to want to hang around the St. Thomas area, but I soon realized it was not to find employment. Just why he was dragging his feet, I was not to understand until much later. In fact I had a great deal to learn about the ins and outs of this man's mind.

We moved our anchorage from Little St. James Island to Greater St. James where Dennis worked on *ROSA*, replacing the broken impellor. He had an extra one for he tries to keep spares of most items that often need repairing or replacing. While he worked on the engine I created some shelving for my clothes using duct tape and the cardboard boxes I had brought with me as luggage. My closet was to be the space behind the fold down back of the small settee; an area measuring two feet in height, five feet in length and only twelve inches in depth. It was to contain ALL of my clothes. Because it was so tiny I had to roll everything to fit them in.

The next day we motored to Compass Point and anchored in water that was shallow and muddy. Dennis had no intended plans but to simply "go and do". Which we went and did. We ran into a couple that Dennis knew, Jack and Lynn, and ate supper with them at a local houseboat café. They took us to look at a nice steel boat they are buying, a beautiful vessel with lots of room to live in. I was jealous. *ROSA* is so tiny in comparison.

During the following days Dennis developed a bad cough. He had a huge medicine bag with everything imaginable in it; lots of things for emergency use if needed while at sea. He found something he felt might help. In the meantime he helped out an old friend by taking her place as the Captain of the downtown Ferry so that she could go to the dentist. I found myself confused by all the politics of the tour boat community in St. Thomas; the backbiting, the vindictiveness of the charter boat owners to their employees. Dennis was not allowed to work for the owners now but he could work for the owners' employees. Huh?

I resented his being sucked back into this irrational kind of life and I told him so as kindly as I could. He paid no attention and did his own thing. And as he did his thing, I did mine which was to wander through the shops and old alleyways of the downtown area, pretending I was a rich tourist and letting the "barkers" lure me into places where I couldn't possibly afford to buy anything. Yet I knew I was no tourist and that my home now was anchored in the harbor and I was ready to move it!

A few days later Dennis's lungs were still congested. The antibiotics had not seemed to help much. Yet he wanted off the boat. We took a bus to the downtown area and enjoyed a pizza buffet. Because we needed the exercise, we chose to walk back. It was almost too much for Dennis for he developed a pounding headache. Back on *ROSA* he napped, sleeping deeply. I used the time to do odd jobs. There is always something that needs to be done.

Dennis had assigned me the responsibility of keeping the Log up to date. It was a tattered and soiled cloth-backed one that he had used for as long as he had had the boat. I promised to buy him a new, beautiful leather bound one for his Christmas present. In it I noted the amounts and costs of the fuel and gas we purchased, plus listing any repairs made. When we start traveling I will note dates and places that we sail to along with any pertinent weather information.

In my own personal diary, however, I noted things of a personal nature. I have become discouraged with each passing day being similar to the one before. I wrote in my journal, and also explained to Dennis, that I did not come down here to finance our living in a noisy harbor surrounded by other boats and in water not conducive for swimming. I wanted to go sailing and see the Caribbean Islands and the sea as he had promised when he asked me to come. After I had my say I went outside to sit on the front hatch cover and talk to God.

It was becoming evident that both Dennis and I are strongly independent people. We came together with separate agendas that we felt were a lot alike. But with our independent natures we each struggled to see and understand the other's view when our agendas clashed. But it was his stern belief that because he was the captain of *ROSA* that he had the final say on *everything*. And that was that.

Through the following years this basic premise would be the cause of many of our problems, assorted quarrels and hurtful grief between the two of us. It would take a lot of mellowing and the passing of time before we could come to a workable compromise that would allow us to stay together and still maintain our independent natures. And yet, staying together was always to be our first priority.

September 29, 2000   St. Thomas USVI

Jeanette in downtown St. Thomas alleyway

CHAPTER TEN

A WEDDING RING FROM A GUMBALL MACHINE

As long as *ROSA* remains in the Caribbean area during the summer months there is always that undercurrent fear of being caught in the path of a hurricane. The formation of one named "Joyce" had been forecast and could be coming our way so we chose to sail to Culebra where there are inside mangroves in which to hide if it does materialize.

We anchored *ROSA* in Dewey Harbor. It's a beautiful place. The local people speak Spanish and seem to enjoy our being here. To occupy my days, I spend many hours doing housekeeping chores. Because I love to create and prepare nice full meals for Dennis and because our galley is so tiny, it takes more time than if I had a larger work space. You wouldn't think so but it does. So with a minimum of an hour and a half spent on each meal preparation, eating and cleaning up afterwards, I don't have much time left over for doing the many other things I also love to do. There isn't much time for my water color painting, reading and sewing. But just being with Dennis makes up for it. It's almost impossible to put into words how deeply we have fallen in love. I know I sound and act like a soupy teenager, but I don't want it to ever end.

It is only in the quiet hours of the night that I allow my moral fundamentalist upbringing to permeate my thoughts. It is then that I acknowledge my regrets that we are not married and in my uncomfortableness, simply place myself in God's mercy.

That evening we moved *ROSA* to the outer bay just behind the reefs that block the rush of incoming waves. We sat out on the deck, absorbed in the beautiful starry night. We both claim a deep religious attachment to God and recognize his basic moral teachings. But something special was happening to us. As the evening progressed we found ourselves discussing this relationship we were now sharing. We felt we needed a more concrete exchange of commitment to each other. Yet for many reasons we have hesitated at the total binding contract that legal marriage requires.

On the morning of October 1st an early rain shower cleared the air. It was my oldest son's forty-ninth birthday today. I wanted to give him a call so we motored the dinghy to the town dock to find an outside pay phone that would work. The call went through easy enough and it was so good to touch base with him. I sent my love to all the family. It has been difficult for me to stay in close contact with them as calling back home is expensive. I still do not have enough knowledge or experience to do the e-mail thing without a lot of help from the cyber-café employees.

We ate an ice cream cone in The Chinaman's Restaurant. In the corner of the outside entrance there was a gumball machine. Dennis put a quarter in and pulled out a gumball plus a small plastic container holding an inexpensive spiral banded ring. Time stopped. Could this be an answer to what we had pondered over the night before? Within seconds and without any fanfare, but with deep conviction, we silently married each other as he slipped the ring onto my finger. We felt the hand of God at work. There were no thoughts of what judgments we might receive from the people back home. Those thoughts might come later but they had no place in this moment. A strange quietness and peace settled over me. Quietness and apprehension settled over Dennis. He

FIND THE WIND

understood what had happened more clearly than I did. But it was done. We were one.

After our evening meal we rowed the dinghy over to a small island in the harbor where we held one another as we talked way into the night of the future we faced.

People come into your life for a reason, a season or a lifetime. When you know which one it is you will know what to do.

October 1, 2000   Culebra Island, West Indies

Jeanette Pickering

Jeanette by the Lift Bridge on Dewey Island

CHAPTER ELEVEN

TEN DAYS IN CULEBRA

How strange to wake up this Monday morning knowing I am no longer a single woman, that I have now chosen to bind myself to another for the rest of my life. The morning was spent in true Honeymoon style with love flowing between one another, sometimes at a gentle speed, then racetrack surges at other times.

This life I am living now is so much like a dream that I often have to pinch myself to prove I am really alive and doing these almost unimaginable things. A woman of my age, having spent a busy life of raising a family, operating a Funeral Home and living the solid, steady life, now having something this spectacular to come my way. Here I am, living on a boat and sailing through waters of such pristine beauty that it boggles my mind and trips my heart.

And yet it is real. I know, for the laundry still has to be done. And e-mails must be sent. Dennis's friend, Richard, who also lives in this harbor on a boat, is building the waterproof box for us, which when finished, we will fasten outside the stern lifeline and use to store fuel for both *ROSA* and the dinghy. Up to now the fuel has been sitting in jugs on the side of the deck right where we have to walk when manning the sails.

Just before noon we went into town to check on the progress of the box. While we were there Dennis did the laundry while I did the e-mail thing. Then we both went to Richard's work shop. It was a haphazard collection of tools and materials gathered under a frazzled tent in a scrambled boatyard. Richard scrounged for a box for me to sit on as we visited. I invited him to come and eat supper with us; an invitation no true sailor would ever refuse.

We rushed home so I could bake a peach cobbler in the tiny oven, and then prepare spaghetti and sauce and cole slaw. My food supply consists mostly of canned goods which we store in bins under the sofa bed. Dry goods like flour, salt, sugar, milk and pasta go in any open cabinet, cubby hole or bin that I can find in the cabin. I buy lots of Bisquick and transfer it from its box to a plastic container. At one time Dennis stored his powdered supplies in Zip Lock bags which conform themselves into the space where they are stored. But after breaking one open and then having to clean up the mess, I chose to use heavy plastic juice-jug containers. Fresh fruits and vegetables are stored in a net bag hanging from the ceiling over the table.

Since the holding compartment in the ice chest is only one square foot in space, very little can go in it. We use Miracle Whip and oleo from squeeze containers that don't have to be refrigerated. Eggs are stored at room temperature, tucked in behind the hanging bag that holds our dishes. All in all I nearly break my arm patting myself on the back for being able to adapt to these testy, trying circumstances and to cook up the presentable meals that I do.

For another week we made Culebra our home port. Because the island is small and the people are so friendly we were able to travel wherever we wanted to go by walking or hitchhiking. We went back to the island cemetery where Dennis hunted for the grave of a friend who had died a few years ago. We never found it.

One evening we watched a group of men fly their model helicopters above a large field. On another evening we joined friends, Paul and Terry on their boat for a shared meal. I always prepare part of the meal to take with us. And on one afternoon, Dennis tried to get Richard to take us out for a sail on his boat. At first he said he would, then backed out. Dennis was peeved yet I was beginning to see a new characteristic in him that I had missed in those two years of letter writing. As the Captain, he wants to be in control of making plans and then he wants those plans to be followed through as he wants them to be.

Richard wasn't putting in much time working on the box. But he was ready to go with us to eat out in the evening. We all went to a political rally one afternoon where they served a buffet meal. After we stayed for the speeches, of course. The speeches were all in Spanish but the camaraderie of the people was quite pleasant. Children and dogs were moving in and out of the crowd having a great time.

That evening Dennis had a disagreement with Richard and decided he would finish the box himself. He had already paid him $380 dollars for the work and it was nowhere near finished. Dennis put on old clothes in which to do fiberglass work and went to the tent to finish it up. I went with him to help load up the lumber he had already paid for and bring it back to the boat. There was enough to make some shelving to replace the cardboard ones I had been using. We motored out of the city harbor to spend the night behind the island reef in order to take off for St. Thomas early the next morning.

Dennis had become restless. There are so many things that need to be done on *ROSA* before we can sail her 'down island'. He has ordered decking. It must be picked up. And we need to refill the propane gas tanks. A hundred things to do. And as I become overwhelmed

Jeanette Pickering

with all the necessary chores that accumulate while living on a boat, I too have become restless. And homesick.

October 10, 2000   Culebra Island, West Indies

Jeanette in Culebra Cemetery

CHAPTER TWELVE

WORK AND PLAY, ALL IN A DAY

This would be our last night on the outer edge of the sweet island of Culebra. We understood it would also be our last pleasant night of rest where the trade winds blow with a constant sweet, soft smell and where the sounds of the never ending waves of surf lap against *ROSA*'s echoing fiberglass hull. The graceful movement of the boat lulled my mind, my soul and spirit all into a single entity of peace. This is what I have been searching for, for a long time.

Culebra! Even to this very day of remembering her, I will have a longing to return there to finish out my days rocking in a boat upon soft, blue-green salty waters.

Capt. Dennis had made the decision for us to return to St. Thomas where we would fill the propane tanks and pick up the mail at the Postal mail drop. Dennis's mother had sent me some long-sleeved blouses that he had requested her to buy for me. He is concerned about the sun burning my skin. I keep forgetting that I am no longer in Missouri but in the tropical sun. He also received some boat parts that she had sent to him. I received a letter from my Missy, propelling me into the reflective mood that usually accompanies homesickness. The mood in turn was reflected in Dennis as he became very tired, very rattled and very impatient with me. We bought groceries and sailed *ROSA* over to Hassel Island, only a half mile or so off St. Thomas's shore line.

Since Dennis is no longer under the stress of everyday employment—I have taken over our financial support so that we can go sailing—he spends time and enjoys working on *ROSA,* readying her for our trip down the Caribbean island chain. He had earlier spoken to a cabinet maker friend, Monty, who has his shop on Hassel Island, about building some shelves for *ROSA*. I had met Monty one afternoon when he had taken the day off and was playing his guitar, sitting in the entrance of the now abandoned Yacht Haven Hotel which was destroyed a few years before during Hurricane Marillyn. So many of these people are from somewhere else, having come to St. Thomas to escape something. Only the West Indians are really what you would call local people.

When we went over to talk to Monty about finishing up the fuel box that Richard had started, Monty was too busy. It would be two weeks before he could even start on it. Dennis was upset. And when he gets upset, I found out, he has hives appear on his body in one place and move around to another spot in a crawling fashion. Amazing and scary.

He likes things done to fit his schedule so the only thing for him to do was to do it himself. He found a room in the abandoned Hotel that surprisingly still had electricity connected to it. He took his tools, lumber, epoxy and glass cloth over to the room and settled in for a few days of carpentry and fiberglass work.

Our evenings became the sweet break time we needed to keep focused on our newly found oneness. We motored the dinghy to the uptown harbor where we tied it up to the boat cleats provided for customers, like a watery parking lot. We ate chicken wings and calamari (squid) at the "Greenhouse", a favorite hangout for tourists. On one special evening we invited the ladies who worked at the Postal mail drop to go sailing in the harbor with us. They had lived all their lives on the island but had never gone sailing. That day while I was running errands for Dennis (forgetting my hat, sunglasses and bottled water, and

FIND THE WIND

almost experiencing a sun stroke) I had picked up some munchies and sandwich ingredients. After work we all sailed to Honeymoon Bay where we swam, ate and watched the sunset. For Cheryl, her little daughter Junie, and Lisa it was an evening of delight. Dennis had worked hard all day yet was so patient with the ladies. The sweetness and kindness he expresses as he talks and tells about the art of sailing boats and ships continually endears him to me. Dennis is a teacher and I was to later learn he had graduated from college with a liberal arts degree. With only another term he could have become an elementary schoolteacher. But then he already is a teacher, and always will be. Just not an employed one.

 Dennis brought his finished box back to the boat. He fastened clasps and hinges on it. I helped him mount it on the port side of the boat, outside of the life line and over the water. He put away all his tools and supplies into the many holds located on the boat. I had purchased a Tupperware-type box yesterday and today I fashioned it into a jewelry box. I cleaned the head area (3' x 2' space) and scrubbed the cabin sole walkway (2' x 8' long) and did a bit of sewing during a break. We spent the day teasing each other, laughing and loving one another.

 That evening we blew our week's grocery money. We took a taxi to the movie theatre on the top of one of St. Thomas's many hills, ate Cracker Jacks that we had smuggled inside Dennis's backpack and then hitched a ride home. Sometimes you can catch a ride. Sometimes you can't. Tonight we were lucky.

   October 14, 2000 St. Thomas, U S V I

Jeanette Pickering

Dennis and Jeanette on Honeymoon Island

CHAPTER THIRTEEN

AN EIGHT DAY COUNTDOWN

The next eight days of our lives served not only to be a culmination of our two years experience of letter writing courtship, but at the end of those eight days there began a roller coaster ride that would not only compete but would defeat any thrilling experience of riding any giant roller coaster that has ever been built.

The best way for me to share the happenings, the untamed, unrestrained and extravagant experiences of those days, and the way they ended is to simply transcribe the words I wrote down in my daily journal; words compacted into an edited version because that is the way I do my journaling. Deciphering the unspoken thoughts that would ordinarily accompany these brief notations, can be left up to the reader of them.

2000, 10-15 Sunday

We were anxious to get away from St. Thomas but I did take the time to bake biscuits and gravy for our breakfast. I truly love cooking for Dennis. We have settled so quickly into this being a couple routine. We closed the hatches, stowed things away and sailed for Buck Island. We found a number of snorkel boats anchored there—the cruise ships are now coming in. We anchored, then dinghied over to a boat called "HAPPY HOUR" and visited with the young couples on it. Dennis knew the captain and had dated one of the girls. After all the charter boats had left we motored around to a calmer side and tied up to two moorings. We snorkeled and watched a lovely sunset from the boat. After working so hard, Dennis is beginning to unwind and relax.

2000, 10-16 Monday

    Today is the anniversary of two years since Dennis and I met—we recalled that meeting several times during the day. We had planned it to be a special day, and it was. I fixed a quick breakfast of biscuits and gravy (leftovers) and we pulled on jeans and heavy shoes to walk to the top of the hill before the sun got too hot. It was a beautiful walk. There are so many wild flowers blooming right now on Buck Island after last week's rains. There was a bank of precious blue wildflowers growing profusely in the warm tropical sun. I would have loved to have had a wedding picture taken in front of them. We climbed to where the light houses were; explored the old one, then climbed up inside the new one. Dennis went to the top, I only went half way. We walked to the grave where a friend of Dennis had buried his dog "Rover'. I had carried an old feather pillow over with us to dump out the feathers. Then I spent the afternoon transferring new feathers into the casing and sewed it up while Dennis visited friends on a Diving Boat. We snorkeled in the afternoon. Dennis fastened the Scuba tank onto the anchor for me to try it out again. This time I did o.k. That evening we shared the blue bottle of St. James wine that I had carried back with me from Missouri.

2000, 10-17 Tuesday

    We had planned to sail back to St. Thomas today yet it was such a lovely day we couldn't make ourselves do it. This morning we ate what we could find in the ice chest, trying to clean it out. We took down the canvas shade-top awning and motored to the twin island of Capella. After slathering on sun lotion we rowed to a surfy beach to walk the whole length of it, gathering shells for me to mail home to the grandkids. By 2:00 Dennis had burned his back through his shirt. I did more scrounging for lunch. We took a nap during the afternoon, and then motored to Buck Island to snorkel. My mask continues to leak. I baked a peach cake while Dennis packed a box of things to send to his mom. We rowed out in the dinghy to watch the sunset, and then snorkeled after dark. What a blast!

2000, 10-18 Wednesday

Knowing that we must return to St. Thomas today we dallied around, not wanting to hurry back at all. It's been such a sweet vacation. But with the ice chest empty and getting low on water, we know we must leave this magical place. But we could still cheat and stay the morning. All the cruise boats were out at our anchorage by 10:00 so we chose to go snorkeling with them. We saw the blue bottle we had tossed on Monday and wondered if someday, someone else might find it and retrieve it. By noon the boats had left. (We had boarded "Doubloon" and shared a beer and a coke with them earlier this morning.) We ate lunch, then put up the sail to head back to St. Thomas. I used the sailing time to write letters to my family (and secretly watch Dennis at the helm of his precious *ROSA)*. We arrived in time to rush to the mail drop where we received an invitation from Cheryl to eat supper with her on Saturday and then we called home. Later I went looking for wedding rings while Dennis ran errands. We ate leftovers for supper.

2000, 1-19 Thursday

Tons of things need to be done, and there is never enough time in which to do them. Most of the time when we are in St. Thomas our lives are lived in a total rat race. Dennis tried to snorkel dive to find our neighbor John's mooring anchor for him. He couldn't find it and had to use his scuba tank. This time he found it. We had planned to go downtown to look for rings, but didn't make it. Dennis packed a box to send back to Georgia. I mended and sewed. We lost a roll of film from Dennis's camera; pictures of us on that first day when I came. It made us sick. We stopped to pick up the two rolls of developed film, laughed at the pictures, then crossed the street and found the wedding rings we wanted. We had to go back to the boat to get the money to pay for them. They are so beautiful. After we bought them, we went to the Pizza place for supper, later stopping at a Recreation bar where we visited with Dennis's friends until late.

2000, 10-20 Friday

Still there are so many things to do and no promise in sight to finish any of them. We have accumulated two big sacks of laundry. One is a full load of cushion covers for the two seating sofas. (The table dropped yesterday spilling food all over them.) I also changed sheets today. As I waited in the Laundromat from 10:00 to 1:00 pm, I wrote letters to Dennis's mom, Loretta, and my family. I also sent Missy checks for payments on my Master card and phone bill. Dennis ran errands, buying a battery for the boat, getting water and ice for the chest. It rained hard while I was folding up the laundry and continued to rain off and on during the day. We counted the balance of the money I had brought with me. We have spent nearly half, which included the cost of the batteries and rings. Not too bad. John had offered to buy our supper as his thanks for the diving work that Dennis did. He motored us down town to a Chinese place.

FIND THE WIND

2000, 10-21 Saturday

Another day, dawning bright and fair, held so much promise as we began sorting our way through it. The morning was for work. Dennis cleaned the boat bottom for our neighbor Harry and had to use his scuba tank as the water was so murky. I sorted the shells and rocks that we had collected on Buck Island, getting them ready to send to the grandchildren. Scott came to the boat to *beg* me to allow Dennis to be on call for him Monday as he is taking over a new job. We laughed and had a good time as I finally relented and said "Yes". Cheryl Thompson came by at 2:00, taking us to her home on top of St. Thomas to swim, eat and watch T V video. I brought slaw and cake. We truly had a delightful time. It was nice to play with her 3 ½ year old daughter. We came home at 9:00, very tired.

2000, 10-22 Sunday
JEANETTE AND DENNIS MARRIED TODAY...

October 22, 2000   St. Thomas, U S V I

Jeanette by Rover's grave

CHAPTER FOURTEEN

THE KEEPING OF WRITTEN THOUGHTS

For years I have kept my diary-journal writings in tiny 2 x 4 appointment books. I carry only the current one with me and store the others in my home in Missouri for safekeeping. During the years I was raising my children, I wrote letters as a means of chronicling my life. Actually I began my diary keeping even before I became a teenager. I had written down my secret thoughts in a small note book which I felt I had hidden. But my mother found it among my clothing and read it. Later for a Christmas gift she gave me a five-year, white leather bound diary which had a tiny lock and key. Now all my secrets were safe. My mother was a wise woman for she knew that all girls have sweet secrets that can only be kept in a *private* journal. And she felt me trustworthy enough that my secrets were not harmful ones.

As my diary keeping grew to become a tool of journaling as well as a holder of secrets, I have been able to use them as I now write my stories. I keep them in a special holder so that they all can be passed on to one of my grandchildren. Hopefully to one who will also be drawn to the love of journaling. I would like to think it would be a granddaughter for I also have one of my mother's diaries and a lovely small wooden box that contains my great-grandfather's and my grandmother's diaries. Precious, precious heirlooms.

However, I never contained my need for writing to just Diary keeping or letter correspondence. I also scribbled notes here and there in spiral bound notebooks and on small pads which I have snuggled all together in boxes and have stored them in an old trunk that a friend gave to me. I also have my mother's writings and poems and her courting letters to my father which he had kept in a black metal box. They are also kept in the trunk.

Now, from my recorded memory, I am able to bring to you these stories of my sailing adventures. For it is from my journals that I kept, where I scribbled and described in deeper detail, that I can share with you the second special day of my second life.

I am a woman who has been blessed with two wedding days to the same man, each conducted in separate, special ways. Here are the recorded thoughts of the second one which were hastily written in the early morning hours as the world around me awakened.

"The morning broke in its golden excellence, creeping over the eastern mountains of the St. Thomas Island. The sparkling gold dust air filtered its way across the sky to the tree tops of the western hillside that rings Charlotte Amalie Bay, sifting its rich splendor over the houses and landscaping. It seems to explode in slow motion. And in only a few minutes the wholeness of the golden sun exposes itself.

A soft eastern wind accompanied the first creeping rays of the light and gently shook out the wrinkles that had creased the ivory shift dress that hung from a plastic hanger fastened to the cross bars of the back mast stays. The dress had been rolled up in a tube-like fashion and laid in the cardboard box shelving that I had created to replace a heavy plastic liner, held by an expanded bungee cord; the only thing available to me for the storage of my clothes.

There was an excitement in the air, a hushed expectancy of an unknown future. For we have chosen today as the beginning of a series of incredulous memories. Today the Captain and I will say our wedding vows.

Other than the dress and the purchase of the two intricately patterned twin wedding bands, no other preparations had been made. Even the wedding site had not yet been chosen for sure but we are leaning toward riding the taxi bus up to the bench on the high hill overlooking Emerald Bay. Two years ago I had visited that spot. I had gone there on the afternoon following a sailboat ride on the *SHADOW*. It was part of a snorkel-swim excursion provided by the Princess Cruise Liner, and Dennis was the Captain of the tour boat. When I was later taken by a tour bus up to Drake's Bench, I was still dizzy from the wild thoughts that followed me after the half-hour visit I had just had with the Captain. Our exchanges of why we were both on this boat at this exact moment had culminated with an invitation. "Would you come and live with me?" As I sat on Drake's bench that day I had been immersed with amazement that someone would see things in me that I could not see and would actually want me to live with him.

Yes, the bench with the magnificent view of the green water that reaches out toward the northwest, far away into the Caribbean Sea, will be a perfect place for us to pledge the unplanned vows. All the thoughts of that unexpected, long ago introduction to one another and all the events that have finally come together on this day of commitment, swirl through my mind as we now prepare to attend today's Sunday morning worship service with Cheryl and Junie at the hill-top Lutheran Church. An afternoon wedding on the bench above Megan's Bay would be perfect."

October 22, 2000   St. Thomas USVI

Jeanette Pickering

Our hands with our new Wedding Rings

CHAPTER FIFTEEN

...AND WE PLEDGED OURSELVES

Cheryl picked us up at the Havensite parking lot a short time before the starting of the second service. It was the service that was mostly attended by children and their mothers. I was dressed in my ivory dress, adorned only with a large blue sapphire pin that I had owned for many years and the blue cat-eye earrings that Dennis had given me for my birthday. Dennis was wearing the white shirt I had brought with me when I came the second time and a necktie he had requested from the numerous ones left by Max when he died.

To some this may have seemed either out of line or even morbid but through our two years of correspondence in which we shared our families and our past lives, it was his desire that my love for Max be included in this new love we now share. We joked as I helped him knot the tie, which turned out too short because of the way I had wound the ends, but it had been years and years since he had worn one, and thinking that this might be the last time he would ever wear another, it would suffice.

The two rings were stored in his backpack, still tucked in their octagonal satin boxes, ready for the afternoon's solemn ceremony. I had not told Cheryl of our plans as I had already explained to her that we had been married in Culebra using the gumball ring that I was now wearing. I also had my camera with me.

The service was nice, geared to the young ones in attendance. There were no fathers in the small crowd. St. Thomas, like many of the Caribbean West Indies islands, is not known for their men to participate too much in family activities, especially church events. Some of the youngsters' parents are not even married.

Following the message, Pastor Spaghetti (his last name was foreign and hard for them to pronounce so he referred to himself by that name) asked if anyone had a happy announcement they would like to make. Cheryl shared with them that Dennis and I had been married a few days before but it had not been in a church. Since a wedding was a special ceremony that only a few of the children had seen performed, Pastor Spaghetti asked if we would like to be married right here, right now, so the children could share in one. "Do you have rings?"

And with my reply of "Yes." he called us up to the front and said to bring the rings with us. I handed Cheryl the camera and up we went. The obviously frightened and off-balanced Captain was undoubtedly out of control of the situation by now. If he had been of a mind to stumble or stammer to object, he didn't seem to have a choice this time. This was it! And the total fear of what he was doing showed in his pale face and his hesitant step as we walked up to where we were to stand.

The vows were the normal ones for this pastor to use. The Captain in his by now confused mind thought he was getting my pledge of obedience to him. But the shared vows were the same, equal in the giving of ourselves to one another in the sight of God and before all these witnessing children who clapped and cheered when we were pronounced husband and wife. We sealed it with a this-is-forever kiss.

Later on in our wedded life we talked about this unique event, the way it came about and the mystery of it all. We have come to this conclusion: we were there that morning because we had chosen to worship God and thank Him for our blessings. He in turn passed on to us

FIND THE WIND

the profound blessing of a marriage that cannot be dismantled, one that no legal divorce can touch.

The ups and downs of our future will follow us in patterns hard to understand. But squabbles and quarrels, leavings and returnings, none of these things can dissolve the pledges we made on that fate-filled morning on a beautiful, sunny October's day.

October 22, 2000   St. Thomas USVI

Wedding picture taken outside the Church

CHAPTER SIXTEEN

GOOD DAYS, BAD DAYS, SWIFTLY PASSING DAYS

In St.Thomas, the seasons of fall, winter and spring all blend in the same as one season; only summer is different in that it produces hotter weather and invites hurricanes. We are now entering the fall season and as the days pass we find that we enjoy doing such simple things together as: packing and sending gifts of gathered shells back home, sitting by the fountain in the park near the Cruise Liner's docks as we eat Hagen-Das chocolate ice cream bars and picking up our wedding photos to relive the joys of that day.

When the circus-noise of the harbor gets to be too much, we slip our mooring and head to Water Island with its beautiful Flamingo Bay. On top of the island there is a WWII bunker. To get to it we have to enter a hidden concrete room just off the beach and climb up through a well-like tunnel using a metal ladder, now weathered and rusting. Today, in a dare-devil fashion we climbed to the top. Once inside we saw it had only narrow slits around the sides, far too small for a person to crawl in or out. The ceiling was low, circular, and had a very thick concrete top. We could see out over the waters that surround the island of St. Thomas and wondered if there was ever a real possibility of this island being invaded. Someone must have thought so.

We ate the lunch I had brought with us and then we very carefully retreated back down the frighteningly deep and spooky chamber to the beach below. Following a road that didn't look like there had been much traffic over it, we climbed up to the top of the hill outside the bunker. We passed an abandoned house with a key lime tree growing beside it. It had lots of fruit, most of it already fallen on the ground, so we gathered up a sack full.

Stopping at an old hotel that had been destroyed by a hurricane, I got out the colored pencils and art pad that I had carried in my back pack and drew the scene looking toward St. Thomas. Dennis created a game for us to play using a short stick and some old salvaged shower curtain rings that he had found. He also found an old rat trap for us to use as we became like small children, amusing ourselves with our imaginative toys.

Toward evening we returned to *ROSA* with plans to play cards after our evening meal. Instead, Dennis began a conversation about religion and beliefs. We opened up for the first time about our religious experiences, how we formed them in our earlier years and also after becoming adults. I was raised in the church of Christ, a very fundamental, opinionated and biased group. Later I became affiliated with the Christian church with basically the same beliefs yet with a more liberal viewpoint. Dennis had been raised in the Baptist and Christian churches. He then later worshiped with his ex-wife and son for seventeen years with the Jehovah Witness group.

As he explained many of his views, I became 'uncomfortable', a word I used in my journal to describe the evening. It was in our conversation that he said that in his last call to his mother she had mentioned that "his wife" (his words) had called her. I was devastated. Not only at his choice of words but that ROSAlinda would still be calling after all the heartfelt-described bitterness he had experienced in his divorce. Only a few days have passed since we exchanged our wedding vows and so soon now I am 'devastated, hurt and confused'. Again, words I used as I wrote of the experience in my journal.

Yet not all evenings and days were ones of discomfort. For on the next day, glancing out to sea we spotted a unique sight; a waterspout, which is a long, narrow, black tornado funnel, out over the water. We watched in amazement as for fifteen minutes or so it moved around and in toward land and the anchorage where Dennis's mooring was located. But within seconds, just before it reached land, it pulled up and into an overhanging black cloud which moved inland to dump a heavy downpour of rain.

Again, it's the little things that give us such enjoyment. We moved *ROSA* to Frenchtown at the west end of Long Bay. I struggle when we keep the boat in the eastern end of Long Bay near the Cruise Liner Docks. There is a strange, unsettled aura that blankets that busy area which affects me uncomfortably. But that morning in Frenchtown, Dennis felt like doing something special; he took us out to breakfast at a quaint little reading café. While we ate sweet rolls and drank fresh brewed coffee, (on the boat we only have instant coffee) he related to me a story of how he was sitting on the steps in front of the café one day and hearing a noise above him he looked up just as a huge lizard peeked over the side and fell right into his lap.

Later we motored back to the mooring. Anchored close to us was a lovely boat with a lovely young girl on board. Her name was Cat and she was a single hander. She invited us on board. The inside of her vessel was a bit larger than ours but with only one person to fill the cabin it seemed even much larger than it really was. I was amazed that a woman could actually be able to sail the Caribbean waters alone. Yet she managed quite well. I wondered if I would ever become capable of doing such a daring task.

The evening, like the one a few days ago, also ended on an unhappy note. As I was helping Dennis put the sail bags away, dropping them down through the round forward hatch, I accidently bumped the heavy hatch lid cover and dropped it on his head. I know it hurt him so much. He became angry and sullen. Again I was devastated and openly cried at my mistake. I continued to cry silently most of the night.

October 27, 2000   St. Thomas U S V I

FIND THE WIND

Jeanette standing by our hauled-out Dinghy

CHAPTER SEVENTEEN

OCTOBER'S END

The up and down moods I am experiencing now are a new phenomenon for me. Not only in the intensity of the highs and the lows but in the frequency in which they occur. I try not to be too concerned but they do throw me off balance.

After a difficult night of silent crying I was glad that Dennis had decided for us to leave St Thomas for a spell, to head east to St. John's and then sail on south to St. Croix. I was excited at the thought of seeing a new island. When I came, it was my dream to see the Caribbean in all its splendor, just as Dennis had described it to me in his letters.

Dennis packed up another of the many boxes that he sends to his mom with plans to mail it at the regular Post Office as he goes to pick up his final pay check. I went to the mail drop with him to pick up the last of our incoming mail. Yet we found that both places were closed on Saturdays.

I walked on up to K-Mart to buy some needed supplies and while I was shopping down in the basement area, the electricity went off. Seems as though this happens fairly often on St. Thomas. They had emergency lighting for us to get out, but they could not ring up purchases at the cash registers. We now had two strikes against us for the day. No mail in or out. No supplies. However, the grocery store was open and I was able to pick up $50 worth of groceries that cost us $100 at Island prices. Patience for the both of us was wearing thin and it was time for us to get out of town.

FIND THE WIND

The anchorage at Buck Island was empty when we arrived. That helped. I cooked a big supper of Bar-B-Que chicken and baked a Key lime pie. The quietness of the evening helped to settle our souls.

Sunday morning found us without a church congregation to worship with so we had a small service with only the two of us participating. As head of the house, Dennis did the reading and *preaching*, with a leaning toward convincing me that his beliefs were the right ones. Sometimes he scares me. But I also express mine and will not be intimidated. Who knows for sure if either of us is right?

At sunset we pulled on jeans and walked through the wild flowers to the top of the hill where the Light House is, to watch the sunset. The sky was filled with the mingled colors of rose, mauve and gold as the tomato colored sun sank below the darkening blue of the sea waters. It was a stunning sight. On our way back down I gathered a hat full of hermit crabs which had tucked themselves into abandoned shells for protection. I dumped them all in the dinghy and watched them scramble and crawl around trying to get out. For so long I have needed to be a child again. And now I have found another child in the guise of an arrogant Sea Captain to be my playmate.

It took us only three hours the next day to sail to Salt Pond on the island of St. John's. There were only three other boats in the anchorage and one of them was a couple who had been Dennis's sailing students years ago in Florida. Small World!

Even with a late start we were still able to make the mile hike across the island tip out to a point called 'Ram's Head'. But it gets dark early here in these islands and night was almost upon us before we could finish the one mile trip back. On this night the waters in this anchorage were not as calm as usual. The boat rocked like a cradle all night. I rather enjoyed it but the Captain prefers a calm, still harbor.

Since we found the trip up to Ram's Head to be so neat last night, we decided to return and make a full day of it. But again, we got a late start, making us climb during the heat of the day. The area is covered with thousands of Turk's Head cactus, big and little ones growing in almost impossible places. A few days before, I had painted a watercolor picture of a vine loaded with mauve blossoms, growing across the rocks. Today I carried my paints with me in my Perusi bag (the one that I had brought home with me from Italy years ago) and found a shade tree under which I could cool off and create a picture of the scene overlooking Salt Bay where *ROSA* was anchored. I paint quickly so I also had time to pull together one focusing on a beautiful red and green Turk's Head growing close by.

During our hike we drank lots of water. We got hot but not dehydrated. The heat here in the tropics really saps the strength out of a person and without a nap, one can quickly wear out. So on our return to *ROSA* we bathed in the salt water, trying to cool off before resting. Even though there is always a tropical breeze, we still have to use the tiny fans to circulate the air inside the cabin.

We had been told that there was a Halloween Party tonight at "Skinny Legs" in Coral Bay Harbor so after our nap, we sailed around the southern tip of the island to search for a spot to anchor in an already crowded bay. It was to be a costume party and we had neither time nor supplies to rig up costumes. But Dennis did create a 'lone ranger' mask and I wore a long skirt. We enjoyed

FIND THE WIND

the evening just watching the others. We did dance some; it was sweet to feel Dennis holding me the way he does…I love him so much that it scares me.

October 31, 2000   Coral Bay, St. Johns BVI

Turks head cactus growing on Rams Head

CHAPTER EIGHTEEN

A FACE TO FACE VISIT WITH GOD

Moods come and go as fast as the mind can travel from St. John's Island back to Missouri, linger there a while and then return back to the Virgin Islands. Noticing that the bottom of the digital clock on the wall at the foot of the bed stated that today is the beginning of November, my mind flipped back sixty-six years to recall my mother's swollen body as she prepared for the birth of my youngest brother. Both mother and brother are gone now. But the homesickness for my still living brother and sister came over me so suddenly, obliterating any concentration of boat-keeping chores and preparation for the exploring of this beautiful island.

I could think of nothing but rushing in to the computer/telephone shop on the east end. First I called my brother Joe. He was so pleased to hear from me. Then I called my daughter, Missy. I opened my e-mail and found a number of incoming notes. Since I pay for the time the computer is in use, I read them quickly and had a number of them printed out so I could take them back to the boat to re-read at my leisure. I guess that's why I've always preferred letter writing to phone calls—the joy that a hand written letter brings lasts longer.

We were able to get back on the boat before the afternoon rain shower began, thus being able to save a number of buckets of rain water that poured from the dark clouds as they passed over the island. The rain clouds usually always come in from the northwest.

The next day was sunny and bright. Using the saved rain water, I washed and rinsed out our pile of dirty laundry using the new soap I had purchased because of the rash on Dennis's sensitive skin. Dennis tied lines from the bow jib-stay back to the double stern-stay, around and back to the bow. That way I could reach up from the deck and hang the longer clothes on both sides of the boat. The underwear and wash cloths were hung over the life lines. Our clean laundry dried quickly in the warm ocean breezes.

By evening the clothes had been folded and put away. It has already become a tradition with us to make sure we watch the sun set. For some reason it sets at an earlier hour here in the islands. It must be because we don't have daylight savings time in St. Johns and also because of our proximity to the equator. Shortly after our supper we snuggled in to our rocking bed with exciting thoughts of tomorrow's commuter bus excursion west across the mountains to the main town of Cruz Bay.

I had never given much thought of ever personally meeting God while on this earth. But on this day, while waiting at the bus stop, He came wandering by. There were a few local ladies and another gentleman waiting with us as we sat on some plank benches. Then without any warning, God, who seemed to be quite agitated as He stomped by, rattled the small bells and seed-filled gourds He had hanging around His neck. He stopped for a bit, just long enough for Him to dispense His displeasure with some of the island's inhabitants.

Being as he was God Almighty, ruler of the universe, it only stood to reason that everything belonged to Him, as the creator of it all. And it was His thinking He should have access to any of the fruit He had provided for a certain lady in her back yard. Wouldn't you think? So when she chased Him off with a broom, He pronounced what He thought was a mild curse on her. She would suffer horrible troubles for the next 365 days, or 366 if next year was a leap year. And then she would die! She should be grateful that He didn't strike her dead today!

And that was how the day began. Yet there were more delights to come.

When the bus finally did arrive, the driver notified us that something on the vehicle was broken, the axle maybe, for the bus was limping along like an old lady. But he would keep it moving and take us as far as the middle of the island where the bus barn was. We could ride with him that far if we wished. From there we would have to find our own way down into the town. With no hope of another bus that day, we all opted to ride at least half the way with him and hitch a ride the rest of the way.

The driver let us out at a small store where we found a fellow that had stopped to pick up a beer. (Rules on driving while drinking are very lax on this island and this fellow was already happy and generous toward hitch-hikers needing a ride.) A few of the more nimble ladies hopped in the back where he kept his buckets of paint and assorted supplies. Dennis had quickly wiggled me inside the cab before the man came out of the store. When the driver climbed in behind the wheel and popped open his can, he gave me the hitch-hiking instructions. The seat belt on the passenger side (and strangely those laws are observed) had a busted fastener so I was to pull the strap over me and just hold it down as if it were fastened.

OK, if that's how it's done. Then, when we took off, the whole seat fell backwards. It wasn't even fastened to the floor! What a ride, flying around the curves, stopping here and there to let someone off, with me hanging on to nothing but thin air to keep my balance.

This was my first introduction to the next hundred-or-so hitch-hiking adventures I would have

FIND THE WIND

within the next few years of my island life. And yet the excitement of such beautiful scenery, such delightful people, along with being enfolded with the magical relationship I was sharing with a romantic Sea Captain, was extraordinary. Almost to the point of being unbelievable. But this was the "Real Thing". And I was loving it.

November 3, 2000

Coral Bay Harbor

CHAPTER NINETEEN

A TREE IN THE MIDDLE OF THE ROAD

It's early November. The temperatures remind me of early July back home. I am told it will always be like this. Even in January. How marvelous!

Up until now we have not left the protection of the U.S. Government. We still remain in U.S. territory. I am a bit anxious to travel to foreign soil but until the Captain, using words of his phrasing, can prove my sailing abilities are perfected enough to be equal to the task ahead, he is hesitant to venture too far south.

However, these islands are still foreign enough for me to hold my curious instincts of investigation and with Dennis's knowledge and experience and like minded curiosity, we shall find enough adventures here to keep me satisfied for a spell.

The town of Cruze Bay on the island of St. Johns is obviously a tourist destination. Shops and eating places are all snuggled around the Ferry docks where visitors arrive and leave every few hours from both St. Thomas and from the British Virgin Island of Tortola. As we were walking around looking for a rental car place, we ran into John, an old friend who had mated for Dennis on the snorkel tour boat. John wasn't the swiftest of mind, living from day to day on a dilapidated old boat in the harbor, which is accessible only by a small surfboard. He wanted Dennis to see his boat and with them leaving me to read the new book I had just purchased, he and John straddled and paddled out to the boat.

The book I bought was actually three small volumes encased in a unique folder box that through time became one of my precious treasures. The books contained the story of two people, Sabine and Griffin, who fell in love much like Dennis and I did. Reading those small books held my fascination for days, opening the pages that held stamped envelopes with letters in them. Very unique.

We later found and rented a car for touring the island the next day. There wasn't much time left in this day as darkness comes early on the islands. We drove the car back to *ROSA*, anchored in Coral Bay on the eastside of the island.

As we left the next morning, we took a side road heading North West. Most of the roads are well paved but with very little parkway on the sides. Only a few minutes into our adventure we came upon a sight that you would probably never see in the States. When they were building the road, directly in the pathway grew a beautifully old tree and instead of cutting it down they divided the road and let the cars pass on either side. I thought, "How quaint. I like the way they think here!"

We chose another road to try to cross the steep hills dividing the north and south beaches. Because of the steepness of the road and because it was not paved but covered with loose large chunk gravel, the tires began to spin and the car began to slide toward the drop off near the edge. I was driving and became very scared. Dennis then got behind the wheel but the same thing happened to him. So we slowly backed down the road in reverse and found an alternate road over to Cruze Bay.

Enjoying the use of the car, we loaded up our empty propane tank and some large pieces of soiled laundry that I couldn't do by hand. We found both a Laundromat and a gas station. But propane fill-ups are done only once a week and this was *not* the day. Later in the afternoon we did get the laundry washed and took it back to the boat in plenty of time to get the car back before the rental cut off time. Hitch-hiking back to *ROSA* was much easier this time. The ride was also in a pickup but in much better shape and the driver was sober in contrast to yesterday's driver. We had a nice visit with him. He too was a charter Captain like Dennis who made his home on the island.

Back on the boat Dennis strung up the clothes lines and I hung up the laundry to let the gentle night breezes dry and whip out the wrinkles that couldn't be ironed out because I didn't have an iron. I had brought a small flat one with me when I came that could be heated on the stove. But Dennis didn't want me to waste the gas and made such a point of it that in a fit of defiance at this unreasonableness, or so I though it to be, I threw it into the Charlotte Amalie Harbor.

I was to learn later that I really did have a lot to learn about the necessity of following Dennis's rules of experience. And being prudent and conservative with propane and water and so many other things, would mean an easier, safer and more pleasant way of sailing travel. Dennis was right to let me learn these things before we started out on our seaward sail south to Trinidad

November 4, 2000

FIND THE WIND

Tree in the Middle of the Road

CHAPTER TWENTY

CARIB INDIAN PETROGLYPHS

We seem to invariably put our anchors down near a port town and then find we can't get away. Dennis doesn't seem to be content to just stay on the boat, doing some of the small tasks that need doing. He continues to have what I call itchy feet. Sometimes going swimming in the salty water helps but mostly he just likes to scratch the itch by walking on land. He flits around like a butterfly and doesn't realize it at all.

Today, because the water in Coral Bay is crowded and isn't clear enough for swimming, we sailed around the end of St. Johns to anchor in Reef Bay. It was late in the afternoon but with enough daylight to row in to shore and walk around the ruins of the old sugar press of the now abandoned Reef Bay Sugar Mill. The tour guide mode in Dennis activates when we find these old historic places and the wealth of information he has amassed through his charter-sailing comes out in teaching lessons. He explained that the huge old tree growing on the compound was a Tamarind tree. The long brown pods hanging from the branches held from one to twelve seeds embedded in a soft brown or reddish-black acid pulp. It is used both medically and in cookery, usually as a relish. Later while we were in Trinidad I saw it sold in Grocery stores and once ate a sweet biscuit made using the pulp as an ingredient. Not too bad!

Just before it got dark, the very tiny bugs we called no-see-ums came out in full force, following us even out across the water to the boat. Dennis has created a unique set of screens for the small ceiling hatches and the doorway entrance into the cabin. He glued one side of long strips of Velcro tape around the frames, and then sewed the other side of the tape onto separate, cut-to-fit pieces of screen-cloth material. We were able to quickly remove the tightly woven pieces from a special made canvas bag and press them on in a jiffy, before too many bugs got into the cabin area. However once we got inside there would be no sitting outside in the cockpit to watch the sunset, which is always a special event of the day for us. The night air soon cooled everything down making the cabin comfortable for sleeping.

  We awoke early, planning to get a cool start for an adventuresome one hour hike up the north trail to a small pool near the top of the mountain. Motionless, it rests at the bottom of a trickling clear waterfall. The early Carib Indians who once lived on this island, cut designs called Petroglyphs in the stones at the back edge of the pool. They are so unique that Goldsmiths have made pendants and earrings using these drawings. I had seen some in the shops that we wandered through while we were in Cruz Bay. Something else caught our attention as we observed these ancient hand carved creations. The level of the water in the pool has remained at the same depth throughout the years, which made us realize there were some designs cut with that fact in mind. A few designs were chiseled right at the water level and could not be observed with clarity. But when Dennis splashed water on them, the shadows of the carving became more pronounced. Then by looking at them from the opposite side of the small pool, we saw one-half of a design above the water and the bottom half of the pattern came from the reflection in the water of the pattern above. This unique planning had come from a very artistic mind of a talented Indian.

As we returned back down the hill, we walked along the trail, merrily chatting away about what we had seen. As we turned a corner, right in front of us was a thin, wrinkled and craggy, elderly dark skinned woman, completely dressed in white, turban and all. She startled us and I guess we must have frightened her too. She quickly disappeared into the scrub bushes leaving us to wonder if she had been real or maybe just an apparition of some sort. Very strange and unsettling, especially in the fact that we were in an isolated part of this tropical forest, an hour's walk away from any civilization.

By late afternoon we sailed west, back into a side bay near the big Cruz Bay. There was lots of boat traffic going in and out of the big bay. Lots of dinghy traffic in a harbor creates continually agitated water, not the kind of harbor we enjoy sleeping in.

About a month ago Dennis had his eyes examined for a new pair of glasses. When completed they were to be sent to his Postal drop-off in St. Thomas. Instead of sailing *ROSA* back across the Pillsbury Sound which separates the two islands, we chose to catch the early Ferry boat over to St. Thomas and spend the day before returning in the evening.

We rode the inexpensive open-air Taxi over to Charlotte Amalie to pick up the new glasses. Also at the mail drop off was a package from Georgia that Dennis's mother had sent containing a few of his snorkel masks for me to choose from. We picked up a new battery to replace one of the two that we use to hold our solar panel power. We were able to hitch a ride back to Red Hook harbor with a friend, Captain Cory. We ran into Peg-leg Jeff again and treated him to supper at the Limnos Bar where we had a delightful visit, laughing, teasing and remembering.

FIND THE WIND

It had rained earlier but stopped around 7:00 p.m. when the Ferry came to take us back to St. Johns. We sat on the upstairs seats, near to the Captains helm. Dennis described the waters as we swiftly motored past the hazards he knew by memory, having captained one of these Ferry boats for a living back a few years ago.

The days continue to be filled to the brim with excitement...and pass by so quickly. I hardly have time to catch my breath. I feel my gears going into overdrive and pushing into overload. I feel I'm going to need some down-time before too long now.

November 7, 2000

Petroglyphs

CHAPTER TWENTY-ONE

FIN-FUN ON A SUNNY DAY

We have had enough of Cruz Bay. It's like living in a fish bowl. There is hardly any privacy. Ferry boats, quarantined boats, supply boats, they all come in and out of this harbor. We spent the morning on land doing laundry, gathering up supplies of fuel, water and a chunk of ice. We like chunks when we can find them for they last longer. During the afternoon we sailed around the west end of St. Johns and by evening had anchored on the north side in Linster Bay.

It is strange how another person's habits can be so quickly absorbed as your own, and especially when two people are as closely joined as Dennis and I are in this little boat. He has always awakened at some point in the night to get up from the bed and eat something or read for a while or even complete some unfinished inside task, and then return to sleep for another few hours. I had to adapt to it when I found I could not go back to sleep with him rattling around with the lights on two feet from my face as he read in bed. I did create a covering for my eyes from a piece of heavy black material, but it became easier for me to just get up and sit on the seat opposite the bed to read or sew. However, this habit I had now adopted was creating a weariness in me that had to be rejuvenated by an everyday afternoon nap.

During the night the weather turned cool. The next morning I was able to do some baking in the tiny oven. The oven heat took the chill from the cabin and with our closing the overhead hatches it became quite cozy inside. I also had fashioned a heavy cloth covering that we could use to cover the doorway. By using a couple of over-ripe bananas to mix in with a cake mix, I was able to bake it into two small deserts. I also baked a pan of cornbread adding whole kernel corn to the batter, just the way Dennis likes it.

There is always an excitement and satisfaction when I prepare our food. And when I place the meal on the tiny lifted up fold-down table, with the red tablecloth that had been cut to wrap around the two steel support poles that protrude through the polished wood top, I am pleasurably content. If I say so myself "I set a nice table!"

We have planned a sail south to the island of St. Croix (pronounced Croy). To alleviate a constant manning of the tiller to navigate the waters, Dennis uses an auto-pilot. He had created a stand to place it on which hangs over the side of the tapered stern. *ROSA* has a canoe-like look. Many people refer to her as double-ended. On the stand he placed the auto-pilot and connected it to the tiller and the G P S. In our preparation for the sail we had checked it over and found it was not working. He took it apart only to find a piece inside was broken. Now we will have to send it back to the factory for repair before we make the long voyage to Trinidad. So much for an easy passage to St. Croix.

Meanwhile, we had a beautiful afternoon to enjoy. It was a perfect time for me to try out the new fins and to pick out a suitable mask from those Loretta had mailed. North of the anchorage was a shallow reef where we could view some fish and corals and allow me to adjust to the new gear. The first mask I tried on leaked. The second one worked. We had such a great time swimming in these pristine waters that we hated to return to the boat, but the air began to cool down fast. After showering off the salt water using the fresh water we carry in our two-gallon shower bag, I pulled on my long cotton gown. It felt good in the evening air.

The next morning, with the rising of the sun, the heat whipped away yesterday's cool air and urged us to take to the water again. We found a cove of starfish, so exotic and unique in their aquatic beauty. Of course I had to have one for a picture. I tried to dive down to retrieve it but couldn't quite get the knack of the flips and plunges it takes to reach the bottom. Even with the fins for added force, my body has just too much buoyancy and inevitably I would drift back up to the surface despite all the arm and leg flailing I could muster. Dennis easily dove to procure one for me. He has had so much experience in snorkel diving, even in deeper waters, and he always swims down to hand-set the anchors each time we drop them.

During the afternoon we rowed the dinghy to shore and hiked up to see the Annaberg Sugar Mill ruins. Only a few people were at the Park today so we were able to tour it with privacy. I had taken my colored pencils and newly purchased purple-velvet art pad with me and chose the cooking building as my subject to draw. Even though my artistic talent is still raw I do want to find time in this busy existence I now live in, to relax and better develop it.

We used the quiet evening to rest up for our long sail early starting tomorrow morning. It's approximately fifty miles but at the five to six knots an hour that *ROSA* makes under sail, the time goes slow. Plus having no help from the auto-pilot, I'm afraid that tiller-minding will become a bit tedious.

November 10, 2000

FIND THE WIND

Jeanette at Annaberg Sugar Mill Ruins

CHAPTER TWENTY-TWO

A FULL MOON SAIL

How can I possibly write down in story form, all the adventurous happenings of our few days on St. Croix? They became only a 'moment' in the moving drama of my Caribbean days. Then when I finally considered putting together a book of the stories I had already written of my travels, I determined it was not to be a travelogue of just places visited and people met. I wanted to add the dimension of feelings; I wanted to add, if I could, an emotional quality in my writing as I coped with this new life. As I kept a daily journal, I had included hints of the inner struggle that was beginning to show itself. But I didn't begin to write my stories until a few months after we had begun our voyage south.

Now as I compile the already written stories and some new ones created from a review of my journal and the Ships log that I kept for the Captain, I have been able to add to them remembrances from the perspective of a few years later. I find I can write somewhat more objectively and still keep that freshness and excitement and wistful blindness that comes with finding a new love, a new sense of adventure.

This would be our first overnight sail away from the boundaries of the only home port I had known so far. It would begin a tumultuous relationship with a man I thought I knew when in actuality I knew very little of the complicated characteristics that inhabited the mind of this fascinating, charismatic and deeply loveable sailor that I had joined myself to. I found myself coming face to face with what I could expect in this companionship with CAPTAIN Dennis. I had to learn what I could expect from him and how I was to react to his expectations of me as we began our lives together.

On any sail of a distance that would require a large number of hours to reach our destination, we would always plan to make it in a night sail. The passage from St. John's to St. Croix began in the evening after dark had settled our world into a peaceful stillness. We both enjoy moments of being away from the company of others, quietly sitting in the cockpit area together. Dennis had chosen to start my lessons of boat handling on this voyage, placing me in the position of being in charge of manning the helm during my appointed time of being on watch. At first it was difficult to switch my mind from driving a car to steering a boat. In a car I turn the wheel to the left to turn the car left. Habits of a lifetime. So when it was my turn to steer the boat, my past conditioning had me doing the same. Wrong move. On *ROSA*, to turn the boat left I had to push the tiller to the right. It took me a while to adapt to this new steering method but I managed to catch on to the concept. Learning to "man the helm" was only a tiny fraction of the necessary things I *had* to learn before the Captain could be really comfortable in allowing me "drive" his boat while he slept.

At midnight he lay down to rest a bit, giving me the watch for a couple of hours. Years ago Dennis had created what is called a 'lee cloth' for sleeping in while we are underway. It is a type of hammock that is snap-fastened to the base of the long narrow seat on the starboard side of the cabin. It is made from blue canvas, stretched horizontally across the front of the seat and fastened by straps to the cabin top. It keeps the sleeping person from falling off the bunk as the boat rocks with the waves. He climbed into the lee cloth and was soon asleep.

Jeanette Pickering

I maintained my watch under a full moon, always mindful of other vessels that also ply these waters in the dark. All boats are to maintain a light at the top of the mast that has a red light on its port side and a green one on the starboard side. It was important for me to remember these details. So I had to devise a helpful hint to distinguish the colors to their position. GREEN – RIGHT – STARBOARD as opposed to RED – LEFT – PORT. One group of words had four or less letters in each word. The other had more than four. That hint worked for me and I could quickly determine which direction any vessel that we encountered was headed while it was still far away.

My watch was uneventful and at 2:00 a.m. it was my turn to catch a snooze. Then at 4:00 it was again my move to take the helm and search for other seagoing vessels. I had to keep my eye on the lighted compass embedded on the outside cabin wall facing my seat, to keep us on course. I soon found this to be a tedious process of sailing and was allowed by the Captain, if I were judicious enough to always to maintain my awareness of the job, to also do some writing. I would use a small penlight as I quickly put down my thoughts as they came. I soon found I was able to enjoy my time at the helm, especially on our much longer voyages when the tiller was hooked up to an auto-pilot and the G P S, freeing my hands from the tiller.

We arrived at Christiansted around 7:30 in the morning where we anchored in an uncrowded harbor. The most obvious thing I noticed was the abundance of floating pieces of sea grass making it impossible for swimming around the boat, besides being unattractive as it often collected floating bottles, cups and trash. We treated ourselves to breakfast at the restaurant-bar which advertized on a big outside sign "FREE BEER TOMORROW". We made a quick sashay around the quaint shops along the harbor's edge to check things out, returning to *ROSA* to catch up on the sleep we had forfeited the night before.

Because our days have by habit rolled into one another, Sundays were somehow similar to any other day. In my past, Sunday had always been a day for me to worship God with other Christians in a church setting. I now found that my only contact with God was prayers to Him from a dumb voice. But this Sunday morning we both seemed to need more than that. Having no clue as to where a church building might be, we chose to carry the Living Bible I had brought with me to the empty shopping mall. Finding a table and chairs in the open center passageway, Dennis began by reading to me the encounter of Christ and Pilate. That day he had the tendency to *preach* to me as he read, as if I had never heard the story before. Whether it was a carry-over of his teaching capacity in his lessons of my learning how to sail or his way of controlling the situation, I didn't know. But I knew I was uncomfortable with it. He allowed me to read to him (after asking me to cover my head, which I chose not to do) the love story of Ruth and Naomi. He had never read it before. Its beauty surprised him.

We made arrangements to rent a car for a tour of the island tomorrow and chose to pick it up that evening allowing us time to drive to a movie theatre before parking the car in a safe place close to the dock for an early morning departure. We considered ourselves lucky to find one for half the cost of the rental car in St. Johns. We also chose to keep it rented for two days.

November 12, 2000

Captain Dennis just before sailing to St. Croix

CHAPTER TWENTY THREE

HOW TO BE A CAPTAIN'S WIFE

Top speed for driving on the island of St. Croix is thirty-five miles per hour. The roads are small and curvy and Dennis had not driven a car for three years. The traffic rules here require the drivers to travel on the left side of the road. It was all a bit tricky, but he did a surprisingly good job.

We drove to the east side of the island where all the well-to-do folks live and where there is an elaborate casino and a huge castle balanced on the top of a hill overlooking the Atlantic. It was a marvelous sunny day and as I rode along with my Captain, I began to learn that he wore his Captainship manner as a covering to the real person that was hidden under layers of struggling through bitter past experiences; his fear of failure, fear of the future, all glued together by his stubborn pride. He also was learning that I was not the wife he had supposed he would find in me. But as we learned these things about each other, it became evident to us we were also building an overwhelming need and love for each other.

The day was filled with laughter, fun, jokes and shared stories as we rounded the south east corner of the island. Following the coastal road, we drove west to the town of Frederiksted. It is an older town, located on a deep harbor and built to accommodate the deep draft sailing ships of the past. It now caters to the large cruise liners that come in each week. Yet strangely enough this town was not as populated with tourists and loud music in comparison to Christiansted.

We toured the old western Fort and began a tradition that we have continued to observe through the years; that of fleshing out the bones of the old historical Forts located throughout the Caribbean Islands. On the same block where the Fort was located we found a modern Kentucky Fried Chicken eatery where we purchased some of the greasiest chicken legs I have ever eaten. We carried our take-out meal to a small, quiet little park built in front of the Fort. Only a few folks had ventured out in the heat of the noon sun. And as usual in any tourist trap, there were a few shops selling souvenirs. I purchased a pink shift dress with humming birds painted on it. Many years later I would recycle the dress into a pillow. It now rests on the reclining chair that graces my upper back porch at Turkey Hollow.

As we motored east on the north shore roads, we crossed some not-too-tall mountains and drove through a local rain forest. We stopped at the Salt River outlet where the claim is made that Columbus landed here with his three boats in 1492. The area is beautiful but the water holds a nasty outside reef. It would be a lovely spot to anchor but the passage is far too narrow for *ROSA* to pass through.

Back in Christiansted we ate ice cream for our supper meal. While we have access to do things that are unavailable while we are out sailing (with no refrigeration, there can be no ice cream) we are prone to overindulge. Between the two of us we ate an entire half-gallon of ice cream. And again we went to see another movie. Having no T V available on *ROSA* we catch a movie whenever we can. We also found that movie theatres on these Caribbean Islands are few and far between.

The Captain is the one who decides how long we will stay on any island. But I knew we would be here at least one more day because of the two-day car rental contract. These are the words I wrote in my journal as we began this day.

"This Tuesday would be one of rushing. The Captain wanted to get an early start again—really early. He also doesn't like cold cereal, and for the life of me I could not get our breakfast cooked, the dishes done and personal hygiene tasks taken care of and be on the deck ready to go in the time he allows. I felt bogged down…but I continued to try. I love this man. I plan to spend the remainder of my days with him, so I shall try my utmost. Believe me, trying to please this Captain has become quite a challenge."

By the time we had left *ROSA*, Dennis's mood had shifted. Today, driving in traffic bothered him. His edginess reverted into bossiness, telling me what to do, how I am to do it, and in general how to conduct myself. During our travel time in to visit the old Winn Plantation, I finally spoke up, explaining to him just how I felt about his accusations that my attitude had flaws in it. This only served to aggravate him all the more. I chose not to let it spoil the day and truly enjoyed touring the old sugar mill with its antiquated wind-power towers, the steam driven engines and horse powered cane-grinding mills. I especially enjoyed the old plantation home, still well maintained and refurbished with the period furniture, showing it as it originally housed the Winn family. One piece of furniture that caught my eye was a special chair that "Massa" used when he came in from the fields. Because it was built with elongated slats of wood that protruded out from the seat, he could stretch out after all his hard labor of "overseeing", place his dirty boots on the foot rests and drink a spot of rum without having to remove his shoes.

Recalling the earlier conversations with the Captain, I felt he would have fit in quite comfortably being a "Massa" on a sugar plantation, sitting in his easy chair, and drinking rum with his boots on. But would I have fit in being the Massa's wife? I don't know about that. I'm not really too sure just where I do fit in being a Captain's wife either. But I plan to stick around and find out!

November 12, 2000   St. Croix V I

FIND THE WIND

Windmill on Winn Plantation

CHAPTER TWENTY FOUR

A GARDEN OF BOTANICAL BEAUTY

The words sailing and cruising are often synonymous in my vocabulary. However the word cruising also denotes, for me, time spent on land. And one of our priorities as we cruised the island today was for us to find a place where we could get our propane tank filled while we had the rental car. Locating places such as gas stations, grocery stores, Laundromats, churches and such has always been Dennis's responsibility. It's one of the most important duties in our sailing experiences and sometimes I tend to forget just how important it is and how much stress has been placed on him as he pulls it all together.

Tuesday we were able to stop at a propane station on our way to the Plantation. We also managed to visit an old cemetery. Dennis had been here before and remembered seeing a monument placed there in memory of a woman who had been buried at sea. It had struck him as unusual, something that he might like to consider for himself. He asked me to take a picture of him standing beside her stone. Which I did. He had such a somber look on his face. Later I was to learn that this cemetery had held some bad memories for him, experienced during a past marriage. Painful ones that he had mentioned but chose not to speak of. None-the-less they had affected his mood for that day.

On Wednesday I had asked for a 'day off' and before Dennis left to go into town by himself, he filled the shower bag and hung it where the sun would warm the water. I was able to shower, wash my hair and then do some writing. On the quiet days, I miss my family and writing letters eases the homesickness. Also I was behind in the postings to my journal and in the Ships Log. Usually it is the Captain's task to write in the log but Dennis has always assigned that job to his mate. I noticed the brief notations that his mother had written during the months she had sailed with him following his divorce from Rosalinda, who had also kept the log in her time.

Since Dennis had been to these islands before, he already knew the special places of interest that he thought we might enjoy together. And his interests are much like mine. We love Botanical Gardens and the one on this island is accessible by using the inexpensive public taxi for transportation. The plants of the Caribbean are extraordinary in their beauty and uniqueness. I was captivated by the configuration and the colors of the Lobster Claw plant. If I lived here, my garden would be filled with them.

I had packed a lunch, which we ate in a shady copse in the St. George Gardens. The tropical breezes, redolent with the smells of the sea as they pass over the shrubs and cactus, the orchids and ferns, had made us sleepy. Shortly after noon we headed back to the boat for a nap. Also there was laundry that needed attention before we could make any plans to move on.

Actually, Dennis makes the plans and then tells me what he wants us to do, sometimes only ten minutes before we are to do it. We had been late in getting to the Laundromat yesterday after our rest and found the place closed. So today it became our first priority, followed by filling both the water and the fuel tanks. We brought the clean wash back to the boat to hang it out in the fast drying sea breezes. I polished off some hand laundry in preparation for tomorrow's early morning departure. Dennis has decided to return back to the island of

Vieques, to the mangroves where we spent our first hurricane together.

It will be good to move on from this place. Even though I have truly enjoyed the sightseeing experiences here, there was a formidable sense of the past that hung over the place for Dennis, causing me uneasiness in my appreciation of its beauty. I'm not sure that I would like to return to this island.

November 17, 2000   St. Croix

FIND THE WIND

Lobster Claw Plant Blossom

CHAPTER TWENTY FIVE

FLAMINGOS IN A HARBOR

We were not ready for the alarm when it went off at 4:30. We were still too exhausted from trying to sleep anchored next to a bar where a live band had played until 4:00 a.m. I fixed a quick breakfast and folded the clothes that had dried during the night. Using what little stamina I had, I helped Dennis pull the dinghy up on the deck, take it apart and hoist the two pieces separately to lower and place them cup-fashioned on the cabin top. By 7:30 we were underway.

Dennis used this 47 mile trip to Vieques Island to teach me my first nautical lesson. He showed me how to plot our course using the compass, charts and the GPS. He included his personal opinion of the false safety of relying on electrical instruments alone as some sailors do. As the hours passed, his lessons continued and I soon found that the information he was putting out was becoming "too much". My eyes began to glaze over and I had to tune him out. He wasn't a tolerant teacher, continuing to push what he felt I needed to learn. I simply ignored him until he finally caught on and slacked up.

It was as if he was driven to share this wealth of the sailing knowledge he was carrying around in his brain. He wanted me to know it even though I might not ever use it. And I probably wouldn't as long as he was the Captain because everything we did was first processed through his mind. He would always be in charge yet he had to teach me all he knew. It wasn't until much later in our relationship that I would understand a surprising truth. If anything had happened to him while we were sailing, I would have to know these things to survive.

FIND THE WIND

We arrived at Vieques at around 2:30 p.m. sailing in and anchoring in the front bay of Ensenada Honda. It was surrounded by U.S.Government leased land that is used for military artillery practice. There are no homes, no people around and the bay was calm, quiet and peaceful. We napped from 4:00 to 7:00, then ate a bite of supper and went back to bed.

At dawn I chose to leave the Captain still snoozing away and went up on deck to catch up on a week's worth of journaling and log-keeping. Earlier the Captain had commented that my log-notations were too lengthy, too wordy. I took his comment to heart and tried to cut down the descriptive phrases but the writer in me just couldn't manage. I told my stories even in the Log-book.

It was a sweet, serene morning, allowing me time not only to reflect on the hour but the season of my life. I pray to God that He lets it continue like this until the end of our time. Dennis says it will. And I believe him. Maybe in the beginning of a marriage all you have to do is trust each other to make it last. I feel so secure in his love. The down days are only tiny pimples on the beautiful giant skin that covers this deep love and respect we have for each other. We chose to make the day one of rest and love making.

Later on toward the evening I baked a pineapple upside-down cake in our tiny oven plus a pan of blueberry muffins. Gas is precious. I bake as much as I can at one heating. The smells coming from *ROSA's* portholes are similar to any that might come from a cottage in the Ozark hills.

I asked Dennis to set up the hand-crank sewing machine for me, and while he read I sewed up four small pillow cases and zigzagged the ends of a new table cloth for our tiny drop leaf table. It was a sweet day from beginning to end. I could get spoiled with this kind of living! The only stress on my part comes in trying to figure out how to handle Dennis when stress works on him.

The next morning I wrote a long letter to my children, describing the day to day sights I see and the uncommon activities I partake of. After lunch we rowed the dinghy over to a wee stretch of beach and hauled the tiny craft in to some small mangrove trees where we turned it upside down and stripped off the old rub-rail that had begun to wear. I helped Dennis as he cut the new plastic hose and fastened it to the edges of the boat with nylon cord. The work was tedious and trying. Plus the occasional rain shower did nothing but stress the Captain more. We finished what we could, and then moved to the sea side of the peninsula, rowing around the reef that protected the bay. We passed three lovely pink flamingos, each standing on one leg. They have been standing on a shallow spot for three days now. We have watched them through the binoculars and they seldom move except to exchange the leg they stand on. It was strange to see them by themselves, away from a flock. We wondered if maybe they might have gotten lost from their group's flight pattern.

On the windward side of the island we gathered shells from the rocky surf to mail back home and then stayed to watch an amazing sunset. Following our supper meal we went up on the deck to sit on the closed round hatch, leaning back against the mast to watch the stars in the dark sky. Often during these easy times, Dennis talks about his past life, giving me hints and clues to a hidden bitterness he carries inside him.

We both felt the need to share who we are with one another. He has a lot of stories to tell me. And I sense a desperate hope in him to pass on the things he has learned from experience and study, that they not be wasted. I was interested in learning them, but he also has to learn that I can take only so much in one sitting.

All in all, nothing spoken this evening could possibly blemish the contentment and peace we felt as we held each other and watched Orion hunt his game across the night sky.

November 20, 2000

Jeanette on Vieques Beach

CHAPTER TWENTY SIX

STARFISH FRISBEES

There was hardly any movement at all made by *ROSA*, tethered as she was to her anchor at the bottom of this calm harbor in Ensenada Honda Bay. The only sound we heard was the surf breaking over the reef on the sea side of this Vieques peninsula. Now and then we would hear the splash of a pelican hitting the water as he dove for a meal.

Since we still consider ourselves to be on our honeymoon, we do honeymoon things. One of the most wondrous things we have found in the joy of our marriage is how we seem to overlook, and even forget, the difference in our ages. Being by ourselves, seeing only the other's face and body as our mirrored reflection, we use each other's acquired wisdom to gauge our own view of things, making us seem identical in age. Today we noted that we have now been married for a month and a day, and as each day passes we continue to fall deeper in love with each other.

By noon we felt it was time to leave the boat for a while. Because there are so many stinging jelly fish in the water around the boat, we rowed over to a deep pocket on the sea side of the island to snorkel where we saw lots of small barracuda fish under the mangrove roots. We also gathered 19 star fish, placing them on the deck to take photos. These beautiful creatures have sucking cups on their bottom sides, like octopus, that tug at your fingers when you hold them in your palms. It's a creepy feeling in a way. Yet like other fish, they still have to stay in water to survive. So in their uncomfortable state on the warm deck, they began to work themselves to the side and off the boat. I assisted them in their return to the water by using a Frisbee-like motion as I tossed them out into the harbor. Holy Moley! Their collision with the water stunned them and for a long while they were unable to sink, floating almost unconscious-like on the water surface.

    I had tossed some of them in the water before I knew what I was doing and before Dennis stopped me. I really felt terrible. About twenty minutes later though they had found their way back to the sandy bottom. Besides nautical lessons I was also learning about the handling and care of starfish.

    Near sunset time we put the motor on the dinghy, grabbed the camera and an umbrella and headed for the northern side of the bay where we saw sharks feeding in the shallows. I was very apprehensive about getting as close to them as Dennis seemed to want to get so we didn't dally long. Chugging along with the big blue and white umbrella opened to keep the quick rain squall from sopping us down, we must have looked a sight. But we were in love. Who cares anyway? There was not another person around for miles.

    This time as we passed the flamingos we decided to see if we could motivate them to move on to where they were supposed to be. They didn't let us get too close but took flight when we were maybe twenty yards away. They were so graceful, stretching out to a wingspan of nearly eight feet. They soared around the harbor about three times and when we left they returned to do their one-legged thing, still standing there when we finally sailed out the next day.

    We were running out of fresh staples so for breakfast on this new morning, I used the left-over apple salad from last night and baked a cobbler using Bisquick.

I don't know how I could have made it through my sailing life without Bisquick. It was hard to find in the down-islands. Tiny, basic grocery stores seldom carry it so I always loaded up when I did find it, sealing the boxes in Zip-Lock bags to always have plenty in supply.

After breakfast I cleaned up the galley and then helped Dennis batten down the hatches. We did not put the dinghy on board for the eight nautical mile trip to the Puerto Real Harbor of Esperonza, Vieques. The three hour passage was an easy one using only the main sail and the #2 jib sail.

All the islands west of St. Thomas are Spanish speaking, which quickly showed me just how much I had forgotten from my High School Spanish Classes of fifty-two years ago.

Dennis rowed the dinghy into town to find a grocery store and buy ice for our tiny ice chest which is our only refrigeration. While he was there he made reservations for a Thanksgiving Day meal at the local Tradewind's Restaurant. When he came back we put the motor on the dinghy and checked out a couple of little islands south of the bay.

Their white sand beaches stretch out in a swoop-like curve. The warm grains clung to our feet as we walked hand in hand across them. A year before I had made it a yoga habit to do a head stand every day. It had been a while since I had tried it but I surprised myself in still being able to keep my balance in a most unorthodox fashion. I still have a picture of me with my head in the sand that can be found in one of my island photo albums.

By evening we had showered and put on our fine clothes. I now wear my wedding dress for Church attendance and special occasions. We found a public pay phone and called home. The park from where we called was filled with local demonstrators, protesting the U.S.Government for using a small bit of their island for big-gun shooting practice off of ships, aiming back to an uninhabited part of the island. Yet they choose to forget that so many of their pay checks come from the U. S. Government, plus the monetary leasing payment for the use of the land.

While we were eating, it rained hard and filled the dinghy. We had to bail it out before we could go back to the boat. It gets dark quickly in the islands after the sun goes down so by using *ROSA's* anchor light located on the top of the mast (we had turned it on before we left) we were able to find our way back home. It had been a full day, with a weary ending. Yet just to hear our families' voices once again put a sweet touch on the dreams we would have tonight.

November 23, 2000

Starfish at Vieques Island

CHAPTER TWENTY SEVEN

CEMETERY BY THE SEA

We would be spending three more days on this island of Vieques, yet we didn't know that when we awakened on this Friday morning. Plans for the day can be changed at the drop of a hat or a barometer so we usually make them as we go. Seldom can we pin-point our days of coming and going.

On the northern side of this island there is a larger town, but by only a bit. However it is big enough to have a City Square with a Park. This morning the Captain suggested we travel across the island to Isabella Segunda to see the ancient Fort that was built there hundreds of years ago. We were able to catch the morning taxi bus over the mountains to spend the whole day exploring the town. We always enjoy the local people we meet but this time we were unable to verbally communicate with them in their Spanish language. Yet it is amazing just how much can be said by tone of voice, pointing and using gestures that are understandable no matter the spoken tongue.

We climbed to view the old Fortress overlooking the north-west harbor, snapping photos as we moved along. Just by looking at how we dress (shorts and tee shirts) the island folks know we are tourists. Plus the way we act as giddy, silly teenagers, they soon figure out we are also honeymooners.

I had not packed a lunch today so rather than hunt for a café, we found a grocery store where we bought some bread, cheese, grapes and a half-gallon of milk. Taking our food with us we ate in the park on the square. The afternoon sun is always hot and strong in the islands so we carried and used the old blue and white golf umbrella that Dennis keeps on *ROSA*.

Randomly choosing a side street to wander along, it led to one of the most unique grave yards that we would encounter in our travels. It was an old one overlooking the sea, which held graves and mausoleums packed in so tightly there was hardly space in between to walk. In a newer section a fresh grave had just been opened. It was dug so deep that we figured it to hold at least five spaces with possible plans for other burials to be stacked in it, one on top of the other. As a former funeral director, I have seen this done only in the states in Veteran's Cemeteries and then with only two spaces per grave, never as many as this grave would hold.

Time got away from us and we missed the taxi bus back and had to hitch a ride. A very friendly local man with whom we were able to communicate by using the few piece-meal Spanish words we knew, gave us a lift in his old battered car back to Esperanza. A small evening shower caught us just as we arrived so we stopped at an up-and-coming outside bar featuring a John Candy movie on its tiny box TV. Dennis loves movies, never met one he didn't like, so it goes without saying we waited out the shower enjoying the whole film. No holding hands and eating popcorn but then few movie houses will serve you beer as you watch their movies.

When a 'free day' comes along where I can remain on *ROSA* in quiet solitude, I jump on it as a chance to write in the Ship's Log, my Journal and letters to my family. Dennis usually heads to town to wander and explore and do his thing. For someone who has been in the habit of spending her days alone as a widow for over three years, I need these breaks to aid me as I cope in this newly formed relationship. I need my space and quiet time; something that the Captain has always had a hard time understanding.

When he returned around 4:00 we hauled anchor and motored to a new harbor, Sun Bay, where we spent the evening playing cards. The only game Dennis knows is his version of Crazy Eights.

"I'll deal out the cards and teach you as we go." he tells me. And that's how I learned the only card game we ever played throughout our next five years of Caribbean sailing. I tried to teach him how to play Cribbage using a book of Card Game Rules that I found on a book-trade shelf in some Marina somewhere. But after only a few tries, the whole process became just too complicated. "This is like work, Jeanette. Let's go back to Crazy Eights." And so we did.

On our last day in Vieques, we let *ROSA* serve as our "House of Worship" with the Captain in charge, preaching the story of Daniel as if he thought I had never heard the story before and as always with a J. W. slant. When it was my turn to read, I was ready to read a chapter of "softer" verses. But by then he was ready to go exploring. We walked back across the beach to Mosquito Bay, gathering shells, laughing, having a sweet time.

I was so in love with this charismatic Captain that I was unable to see the manipulative character that was slowly emerging from him in such a soft, sly manner as he attempted to control our lives together. But because of my soft, very independent manner, he was having a hard time of it. How many times did I wonder if he wondered what was really happening to us…this slow building of a love that would never, ever die.

November 26, 2000   Vieques Island

FIND THE WIND

Jeanette at the Vieques Cemetery

CHAPTER TWENTY EIGHT

CLOTHING OPTIONAL

The only thing I regret about our stay on Vieques is not finding the phosphorescent bay that someone had told Dennis was there, despite our feeble attempts at asking the locals for a location.

But today is a new day. The alarm had been set for 7:00 a.m. The radio weather forecast was for a 50% chance of rain. Moving quickly we closed down the hatches and hoisted up the anchors, (Dennis always sets two), and sail-glided out at 8:30. I am to meet Missy in San Juan on the first of December for us to board the Princess Cruise Liner for a one week cruise around the Caribbean Islands. We had planned and paid for this cruise long before I ran away from home. This might be my last chance to share some special time with her.

We thought about stopping to snorkel on the north side of Vieques on our way out but because the weather was shaping up exceptionally good today, we dropped that plan. The Captain continued with his sailing lessons, putting me in charge of the helm for long stretches at a time. There is no shade while manning the tiller and I picked up a bit of sun, burning my nose. Dennis has begun to develop a sore throat and was not feeling well. We traveled 26.4 miles across the Vieques Sound, sailing around the north side of the small island of Isla Palominos which is just across from the Puerto Rican harbor of Fajardo.

At 3:30 we arrived in the harbor that accommodates the ferry boat from the big gambling casino in Fajardo. They also own a large hotel complex on this island. Dennis used two empty moorings balls to try to avoid the obvious rolling of the sea expected this evening. The trip had really zapped us so we were too tired to even put the dinghy in the water. It takes a lot of time and energy to untie, lift, hoist, bolt together, hoist again and swing the boat over the life lines to lower it into the water.

I fixed some quick soup before we napped. After darkness had erased out the daylight, we finally roused enough to listen to the evening weather forecast. It didn't sound good. When the forecast came on the next morning it proved we were in for a rough day. The wind blew all day, sometimes quite fiercely. There were showers off and on all morning and with Dennis hating rain as he does, he was moody, grumpy and snappy with me. He had no medication for his sore throat and on this tiny boat there is no privacy space to hunker down in when you don't feel well. In his view I was being "aggravating". I chose to hush and write, filling my journal with these words:

"I try hard not to upset the Captain. But he has made such a change in my life as I try to accommodate him. Yet it is the little things that I seem to be unable to remember and master...things like not shutting the cabinet doors as I prepare a meal, leaving drawers open, forgetting to shut off the gas at the tank connection when I am through, leaving stuff on the bunk and cabin seats—all hurtful and dangerous. And I know it. I seem to be a bit lost. And sad."

In the afternoon Dennis got out the sewing machine. (The former owner's name is boldly written on the handbook cover). He sewed up a knife sheath for the kitchen knives. He hardly touched me today, says it is his sore throat. And he hinted that he was homesick. I wondered but guessed for whom…and quietly pushed down the jealousy I feel forming inside me, of someone or something I cannot put my finger on.

Just before sunset we un-decked the dinghy and motored to shore for a breather. As we walked on the soft beach sand there was a chill in the air, and also in the Captain's mood. A malady that could become contagious if I let it.

Daybreak is my special time of the day to go up on deck and write. It also allows the Captain to stretch out over the tiny twin-sized fold-down bunk bed. After logging in necessary notations in the Ship's Log and jotting private thoughts in my Journal, I fixed biscuits and gravy for breakfast before we motored over to the Conquistador restaurant for a cup of fresh perked coffee. (We drink instant coffee while on *ROSA*.) We hiked on the island's only trail, overgrown with creeping thorn plants. Dennis is feeling better today.

On the east side of the island was a "clothing optional" beach where I chose to strip down and go swimming. There were no other people there yet. I did more rolling in the surf than swimming, finding the undertow quite strong. Dennis walked the beach, gathering discarded water bottles to cut in half to use for deck repair work.

Back on the boat we prepared for a quick afternoon sail of four miles across the sound to Puerto Rico to find a suitable place to leave *ROSA* while we make our way into San Juan where we are to meet Missy at the airport.

Our arrival at the Fajardo Harbor at 3:00 p.m. should have been a slow time for the Marinas but there was still a fair amount of traffic. Even though there were lots of marinas and docks, empty and suitable places for *ROSA* to tie down to were hard to find. Dennis was stressed and developed a headache. It had taken us more time than we had planned.

The day fast became night. Tomorrow we will find a rental car...but not this evening.

November 29, 2000

Jeanette Pickering

Jeanette on Clothing Optional Beach

CHAPTER TWENTY-NINE

A PUERTO RICAN PARTING

Thursday, Friday, Saturday. Three more days before I am to be separated from Dennis. Thoughts of the separation do not trouble me but they do place me within the same wordless emotions that every woman faces when she knows she will be without the touch, the sound and smell of her love for a length of time. A day or a year.

In our case it would last only as long as the remainder of the year with plans for us to reunite at his mother's home in Georgia where we would celebrate the New Year's beginning. It would only be a month's duration but to us it would seem a lifetime. The next three days would be precious ones.

There were so many chores to be done before I left *ROSA*. Laundry to do. Groceries to buy. And while we had a rental car, places to see. A few years ago, when Dennis's mother had sailed with him, they had visited the Yanki Rain Forrest on this eastern side of Puerto Rico. He wanted me to explore it with him. But we both knew there would not be time to do all the hiking we wanted.

As it turned out, the main trails had been closed for repair work, so plans to climb to the very top to the Tower Peak, had to be cancelled. Plus, it rained off and on the whole morning. I was content just being with him. "We'll come back here again at another time" he told me, knowing that we probably never would. But it satisfied us.

Dennis would need groceries for his few weeks' stay on *ROSA* as his plans were to sail her back to St. Thomas and leave her on his mooring in the Charlotte Amalie Harbor while he flew back to Georgia for the last two weeks of December. We found a big-city grocery store, the first one we had access to so far, and loaded the car with supplies and canned goods for our eventual sail to South America. It was my first experience in shopping big-time with the Captain. It gave me a lesson in how to choose food and fill the cart with as much as you could in the quickest time possible. Slow, take your time shopping, the kind I am used to, is no longer an option. Later I would learn that time and transportation would be the criteria for any future grocery shopping.

Since *ROSA* was now tied up in a dock slip, we carried our groceries and ice back from the parked car in a wheelbarrow provided by the marina. Then we carried our laundry and soap back to the car to go search for a large laundromat since the tiny one-tub wash room in the marina was closed. Surprise! We found the laundromats in Fajardo were also closed...we had waited too late thinking we needed a short nap together before we left to go do laundry. Now Dennis was stressed again, his headache had returned and I cried because I didn't know what else to do.

After a restless night, the morning found us both nervous, on edge, but excitedly happy. Dennis would be meeting Missy for the first time and the apprehension was thick. Yet we still had to get the laundry done. We talked it over and decided that when we did get it finished, we would not take it back to the boat. He would take care of it later.

There was a Post Office in the same complex as the laundromat, which gave us the opportunity to mail back home a box of shells I had collected during the past two months. And Dennis needed to send his auto-pilot back to the factory. We drove straight to the airport to make sure we could find the right terminal before we stopped to grab a bite to eat. We made a wrong turn, got lost and wasted precious time hunting for the terminal. There was no time left to eat.

Missy's plane had arrived right on time. It was such a joy to greet her and introduce her to my new life companion. Dennis was like a kid. He couldn't be happier. He and Missy became friends immediately.

We decided to leave the car at the hotel where we were to spend the night and walk up to the Old San Juan Fort and the Cemetery, El Moro. By the time we had taken a quick tour of the place it was late afternoon. Since we hadn't eaten lunch, we bought a fast food meal and ate in the park, watching the people, mostly tourists. We chatted away fifty to nothing until the sun went down.

Back at the hotel, Dennis took a long tub bath while Missy and I had a drink in the hotel's outside patio, catching up, and nailing down our plans for the next week's cruise through the Islands north of South America and the Islands of the eastern Caribbean.

We returned to our room to find that Dennis had finished his leisurely soak and was dressed in his night clothes, including the socks which he always wears as he sleeps, even for naps. Stretched out on the second bed, watching TV, he looked more like a teenager than a seasoned sailor. The socks, long white tube ones, were tattooed with a fish eye logo that he had crafted with a felt marker. It was a simple V pointing outward from the toes with a dot in the center.

Missy quizzed him as to its meaning. I too had been curious but had never asked. It seems that the Captain has a propensity for stubbing the toes of his big flat feet and some mysteriously minded lady had told him that the fish-eye logo would keep him from bumping into stuff. He swears it has helped him. Sounded quite reasonable to him.

Saturday morning would be my final day with Dennis. Missy and I packed our bags and had them waiting outside the door of our room at 9:00 a.m. to be picked up and transferred to the cruise ship. The three of us ate our breakfast in the hotel dining room where Dennis and Missy continued with their jovial back-and-forth banter. I am so pleased they have hit it off so well, and pray that my boys will also accept him as quickly as Missy has. It is important to me that they do for he is now a part of my life. And I am in his.

And thus, near the noon hour, I left him, running like a young boy alongside the bus as it pulled out, waving and blowing kisses. Oh, if forever it could be so…this special bond we now share at this very moment.

These past three months have been like a dream for me. But now, in reality, they were only actual experiences of a condensed lifetime. Anything the future might bring in emotional form has already been accomplished from high to low. Only the activities will change as my existence as a single woman moves on to sharing events in a joint experiment in living. Places to go. Things to see. People to meet. It will all be brilliantly new and keenly felt.

December 2, 2000   Puerto Rico

FIND THE WIND

Old San Juan, Puerto Rico Cemetery

www.ingramcontent.com/pod-product-compliance
Lightning Source LLC
Chambersburg PA
CBHW071211070526
44584CB00019B/2997